f the two Places which comes first in Alphabe
expressed. Thus, to find the Distance from
where the Lines meet is found 90, the distance

Lakes (Kendal)	Lyne Regis	Lymington	Malvern	Margate	Matlock	Ramsgate	Scarborough	Southend	Southampt	Swansea	Teignmout	Tenby	Tunbridge	Weymouth	Worthing	Yarmouth
05																
00	79															
36	128	134														
32	217	161	190													
23	209	186	87	215												
1	215	157	192	5	213											
22	329	299	213	287	117	288										
06	187	139	164	117	171	110	235									
6	75	13	118	154	172	150	284	121								
7	150	181	111	275	200	271	301	251	163							
1	44	139	138	257	235	253	356	231	124	173						
6	192	222	245	314	241	310	343	293	205	53	219					
9	160	101	141	64	179	61	251	81	84	238	220	291				
3	26	54	134	205	204	202	315	172	60	157	73	210	146			
5	126	50	166	108	202	104	282	103	64	210	182	263	40	111		
8	267	216	213	199	188	200	251	104	202	311	307	364	162	253	184	

THE ENGLISH GUIDE BOOK

c 1780—1870

An Illustrated History

JOHN VAUGHAN

DAVID & CHARLES

NEWTON ABBOT   LONDON
NORTH POMFRET (VT) VANCOUVER

0 7153 5996 7

Set in 11 on 13pt Imprint by Avontype (Bristol)
Limited and printed in Great Britain by Biddles Ltd
Guildford for David & Charles (Holdings) Limited
South Devon House Newton Abbot Devon

Published in the United States of America by
David & Charles Inc North Pomfret
Vermont 05053 USA

Published in Canada by Douglas David & Charles
Limited 3645 McKechnie Drive
West Vancouver BC

Contents

List of Illustrations

INITIAL LETTERS

3. Advertisement block: Croall's Royal Mail and General Coach Establishment

Preface

'Guide-books are worthy of study in their own right, as a form of human activity; if few of them possess literary merits of high rank, many of them fulfil to a remarkable degree the purposes for which they exist. They have special claims on archaeologists, historians, and antiquaries; they may provide information, sometimes as the most accessible, sometimes of the best, or even the only, sources, not merely for the history of monuments, but also for the social and economic life of the past, and occasionally for its modes of thought. But individual books cannot be properly used for these purposes if isolated from their fellows . . .' wrote E. S. de Beer in 1952, in an article which sketched the origins of the guide book. *The English Guide Book c1780–1870* takes up some of the points raised by Esmond de Beer and explores some of the idiosyncrasies of the English guide book until its formalisation in the second half of the nineteenth century.

The main source has been my own collection, from which I have taken most of the illustrations and extracts, but I am grateful to local history librarians who have kindly lent books in their care for my use. The other collections to be consulted extensively are those of the British Museum, and the Bodleian Library, Oxford. A comprehensive bibliography has not been attempted but the notes contain references to sources valuable to collectors and others, though many of these books may not be easily accessible. Although incomplete, J. P. Anderson's *The Book of British Topography* (1881) remains indispensable.

Friends and colleagues have been generous: for their wise counsel and kindly guidance I am particularly indebted to J. J. Bagley, D. Birch, T. S. Broadhurst, and W. E. Marsden of the University of Liverpool, and to Paul Morgan of the Bodleian Library. Without the encouragement and long-suffering patience of Dr Brian Harley of the University of Exeter nothing would have been achieved.

From those into whose specialist fields I have trespassed, I ask forgiveness.

J.E.V.

Rodney Street
Liverpool

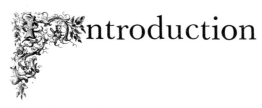ntroduction

A guide book makes certain presuppositions: first, that there are places of sufficient interest to be visited by the stranger; second, that there is an author with local pride; and third, that a tradesman is willing to speculate that these two are worth bringing together in a book. The purchase of a guide may indicate a certain lack of sophistication[1] in a reader, but it also points to a mind sufficiently alert to demand information and to a person with the leisure and economic power to satisfy this curiosity.

The growth and development of the English guide book followed the economic and social patterns of the life of the country. On rare occasions the guide book may even claim to have stimulated change. In the end it was the victim of these developments, since the quality of its production declined with the general fall in the standards of mass-produced books in the later decades of the nineteenth century. Possibly further reasons for its decline were the failing fortunes of the commercial lending libraries, one of the principal agents for the publishing of guides in the earlier decades of the century, and the temporary faltering of such firms as Adam & Charles Black in the face of editorial problems, particularly the need to revise their guides regularly. Success in the genre tempted some publishers to produce hack work of very little merit.

THE

HASTINGS GUIDE;

CONTAINING

A DESCRIPTION OF THAT ANCIENT TOWN AND PORT,

AND THE

Romantic Scenery in the Environs:

AN ACCOUNT OF THE

Antiquities,	Fisheries,	Ruins,
Castles,	Fortifications,	Trade,
Churches,	Gentlemen's Seats,	Walks, Rides,
Fairs,	Markets,	

AND LODGING HOUSES ;

ALSO,

THE TIMES OF GOING OUT AND COMING IN OF

THE COACHES, POST, WAGGONS, HOYS, &c.

WITH A

Table of the Distances from Hastings to Places Adjacent.

TO WHICH IS ADDED, AN

ACCOUNT OF THE CINQUE PORTS,

AND A MINUTE DETAIL OF THE FAMOUS

BATTLE OF HASTINGS.

————◆————

THE FIFTH EDITION.

WITH PLATES.

————◆————

Hastings:

PRINTED FOR J. BARRY, MARINE LIBRARY.

———

1821.

4.   *The Hastings Guide:* title page

CHAPTER ONE

Travellers and Travelling

Broadening of minds

The motives for travel are various: piety, curiosity, trade, health or education. Encouraged by the granting of indulgences, medieval pilgrims set off for distant parts.[1] A twelfth-century guide for pilgrims to St James of Compostella, containing lists of stages and towns between the Pyrenees and Compostella with accounts of the inhabitants of the country, has notes of rivers to be crossed and of relics along the road. This form of guide was adaptable for the use of other serious travellers, with additional descriptive material for those with more leisure and with different interests. In place of shrines and relics there were gentlemen's houses to be seen, and their furnishings, chiefly their pictures. Culture superseded piety as the excuse for making a tour.

In England the search for physical health as a motive for excursions certainly existed in the Middle Ages. Early in the seventeenth century the term, 'spa', or 'spaw', began to have general application. It was originally the name of a watering place in the province of Liége, Belgium, celebrated for the curative properties of its mineral springs. Pre-eminent among the British spas is, of

5. *A Guide to All the Watering and Sea-bathing Places:* the Pump Room, Bath

course, Bath, the Aquae Sulis or Aquae Calidae of the Romans. The hot springs were the mythological discovery of King Bladud. The site was never entirely deserted and by the sixteenth century the citizens seem to have realised the possibilities of an entertainments industry. Pleasure seekers were mingling with the sick. John Evelyn, for example, paid what may be called a holiday visit in 1639. The attractions of the inland spas were promoted by such physicians as Dr Thomas Johnson (died 1644), the author of *Thermae Bathonicae*. Increasing demands from the leisured classes needing cures led to the discovery of more than 100 different sources of waters with varying properties between 1660 and 1714. Examples are Clifton, Harrogate, Tunbridge Wells, Epsom, Scarborough, Leamington, Cheltenham, and (a late developer) Malvern.

Royalty apparently accepted the view that the conception of a child was aided by taking the waters, and such extravagant claims were not unusual.

The celebrated uses of Bristol Hotwell water are to temper an hot acrimonious blood, to palliate or cure consumptions, weakness of the lungs, hectic fevers and heats. It is successfully prescribed in uterine and other internal haemorrhages and in inflammations, in spitting of blood, dysentery, immoderate flux of the menses, in the fluor albus, and perulent ulcers of the viscera. It is of great use in old diarrhaeas, in gleets and especially the diabetes for which it is particularly extolled; and in other cases where the secretions are too much increased, and the humors too thin; in the stone and gravel, and the stranguary; in colliquative sweats, in nervous atrophy, in scorbutic and rheumatic cases, in colics, the gout, loss of appetite and indigestion, in the venereal disease, and both internally and externally in cancers and the king's-evil. In these disorders Bath waters are not only improper but hurtful.[2]

6. *The Original Bath Guide:* Assembly Rooms

7. *A Guide to All the Watering and Sea-bathing Places:* Tunbridge Wells

Gradually the holiday element triumphed and spas became centres of fashionable diversion. For example, in *The Original Bath Guide* there are the usual descriptions of the virtues of the waters, but they form a relatively small section and social concerns are increasingly prominent. The gay social round of the period is recorded by the novels of Jane Austen and others as well as in such satirical poems as Christopher Anstey's *New Bath Guide: or, Memoirs of the B-n-r-d Family in a Series of Poetical Epistles.*[3]

Early in the seventeenth century the virtues of sea water were thought to be a substitute for those of the inland spas, and by the beginning of the next century the custom of sea bathing was so accepted as to become a possible subject for taxation. At about the same period, a 'season' became established and further medical publications, such as Dr Richard Russell's *Dissertation on the Use of Sea Water* (1752), helped to create a demand that led to the birth of new resorts on the coast or the development of existing fishing villages, which were to grow into formidable rivals and eventually into supplanters of the inland spas, although not before almost every mineral spring in England had acquired its followers.[4]

William Cowper (1731–1800) recorded the changing fashion in his poem 'Retirement' (1782).

> Your prudent grandmammas, ye modern belles,
> Content with Bristol, Bath and Tunbridge Wells,
> When health required it would consent to roam,
> Else more attached to pleasures found at home.
> But now alike, gay widow, virgin, wife,
> Ingenious to diversify dull life,
> In coaches, chaises, caravans and hoys,
> Fly to the coast for daily, nightly joys,
> And all, impatient of dry land, agree
> With one consent to rush into the sea.

Sea bathing was a very serious matter and Dr Russell warned that though 'Sea-water is endued with many and great Virtues, the Unskilful may make a very bad Use.' It was also a fairly strenuous operation. It was thought ess ntial that the pores should be closed before entering the water, and so the colder the atmosphere the better. Bathing early in the day was advised. In Fanny Burney's *Diary* there is an account of her bathing at Brighton with Mrs and Miss Thrales in November 1782. 'We rose at six o'clock in the morn and by the pale blink o' the moon went to the seaside where we had bespoken the bathing-women to be ready for us, and into the ocean we plunged. It was cold but pleasant. I have bathed so often as to lose my dread of the operation.' Sea bathing was made a decorous pastime through the invention of the bathing machine by the Margate Quaker Benjamin Beale, in the 1750s. His device had a canvas screen or hood which would be furled when not in use.

8. *Wallis's Brighton:* the Chain Pier

The machine was trundled down the beach into a sufficient depth of water, with the prospective bather inside. At the appropriate spot the driver let the hood down by pulling a string and the bather

9. Bathing machines: wood engraving by G. W. Bonner

20

entered the water unobserved. These machines were adopted by other resorts, but not universally, for Granville in 1841 thought their absence from Brighton a stain on that town's gentility.

His comments illustrate the fact that some travellers could be critical. One critic was Mrs Priscilla Wakefield (1751–1832), the Quaker philanthropist, who produced school books, including one on geography called *A Family Tour Through the British Empire* —a tour 'for the sake of collecting useful knowledge'[5] and not amusement. It was also undertaken to benefit the health of one of the children, but Mrs Wakefield did not propose to visit the spas as these 'form the habits of idleness and trifling'. On the other hand, John Feltham, the editor of a *Guide to Paris* and *Picture of London*,

10. *The Milton and Gravesend Guide:* Bathing Establishment

GREAT SOUTHERN & WESTERN RAILWAY.

SUMMER EXCURSIONS.

KILLARNEY, &c.

On and after the 23rd instant, until the 30th of September next,

First and Second Class Excursion Tickets

Will be issued daily, at the King's-bridge Terminus,

FROM DUBLIN TO KILLARNEY AND BACK,

By Rail to Mallow, and thence by Coach to Killarney.

FARES		£	s.
First Class and Inside Coach		2	8s.
First Class and Outside Coach		2	0
Second Class and ditto		1	12

These Tickets will be available for return within FOURTEEN DAYS after the day when issued.

N. B.—Parties residing in the country can, by applying to G. E. ILBERY, King's-bridge Terminus, Dublin, and remitting the amount of fare, be supplied with Excursion Tickets, which will enable them to join the trains at the stations nearest to their places of residence.

By Order,

WILLIAM TAYLOR, *Secretary.*

Offices, King's-bridge Terminus,
Dublin, 20th June, 1849.

11. *The Stranger's Guide Through Dublin:* GS & WR excursions
   advertisement

defended those 'who seek harmless amusement in travel, or who make temporary retreats from business, in order to return with fresh vigor of body and of mind, to the duties of their station' in the preface to his compendious *A Guide to All the Watering and Sea-bathing Places,* first published in 1803.

Growth of leisure

For those who had no need to work, there was the problem of leisure, especially acute on Sundays. Lady Greville wrote at the end of the nineteenth century: 'Sunday has long been rather a stumbling-block in England to those who love to amuse themselves, it does not appeal much to Society at large, for a day of enforced rest to people who never have any work in particular to do loses all *raison d'être*.'[6] Respectable writers, such as Thomas Kirkland Glazebrook (1780–1855) in his *Guide to Southport*,[7] tended to view with disfavour the exuberant method of enjoying a Sabbath by the seaside indulged in by some visitors. Steamer excursions from London to Ramsgate were jolly affairs that would probably not have pleased him. The first railway excursion to be publicly advertised and sponsored by an agent, however, was Thomas Cook's famous Leicester to Loughborough temperance outing in July 1841.

Until the Bank Holidays Act, 1871, the dangers of the humbler classes going far was slight, although workers might tramp seeking seasonable occupations. Employers were not generous in providing leisure for their employees. Sunday was a day of rest, and Christmas and Good Friday were both legal holidays; but Boxing Day, Easter Monday and Whit Monday were only allowed by generous masters. After the Act of 1871, promoted by Sir John Lubbock (hence the early title for the new holidays as 'St Lubbock's Days'), the immediate impact was slight. Although many public offices closed, business went on much as usual in the first years of the Act. In Regent Street only twelve shops shut and *The Times* gave a gentle hint to West End shoppers to be more considerate. The working of the Act was made easier by the Holidays Extension Act of 1875, which extended the earlier Act to docks, customs houses, inland revenue offices and bonding warehouses. Lubbock's continued struggle led to the Shops Hours Regulation Act in 1886, which restricted the working hours of shop assistants under eighteen to 74 a week. It was 1904 before he managed to push his principal Early Closing Act through the House of Lords. Although there was a massive increase in excursions, these were mainly confined to

SOUTH EASTERN
PAVILION HOTEL,
FOLKESTONE.

PAVILION ARRANGEMENTS.

It is particularly requested that no Fees will be offered to any of the Servants of this Establishment.

The Servants of the Establishment are not allowed to receive any Fees or Gratuities whatever from the Visitors, but in lieu thereof, one shilling and sixpence will be charged to each Visitor for attendance for the first day, and one shilling per day afterwards; and to a family of more than three persons, half the first charge (after the first day).

Visitors having no Apartments in the Hotel, will be charged sixpence attendance for each meal.

From any hour in the morning until TEN o'Clock Breakfast will be ready at a General Table in the Table d'Hôte Room. After TEN o'Clock refreshments can be obtained at separate tables in the Coffee Room. Visitors having private sitting rooms will also be at liberty to take advantage of the public arrangements.

At Two o'clock a Table d'Hôte Dinner will be ready, at two shillings and sixpence each person. During the Summer months, another Table d'Hôte will be ready at SIX o'Clock at four shillings each person.

N.B. Parties wishing to dine at the latter hour, should send their names to the Bar in the Coffee Room before Three o'Clock.

With a view to promote the comfort and economy of the Visitors of the Hotel, a Saloon is Established with private attendance, to which Ladies and Gentlemen will have access upon payment of one shilling each *per diem*, and to those families who have engaged a sitting room such Saloon will be free.

Ladies and Gentlemen visiting this Establishment, are most earnestly requested to communicate to MR. GIOVANINI, the Manager of the Hotel, any cause of complaint that may arise from neglect or want of attention on the part of any one employed in it, in order that the same may be investigated and remedied.

12. *The New Illustrated Hand-book to Folkestone:* hotel tariff

LIST OF PRICES.

HOTEL.

	s.	d.
GROUND FLOOR:—Sitting Room	6	0
Ditto, small	4	0
Bed Room, large Bed	4	0
Ditto, small ditto	2	6
FIRST FLOOR:—Sitting Room	6	0
Ditto, small	4	0
Bed Room, large Bed	4	0
Ditto, small ditto	2	6
SECOND FLOOR:—Bedroom, large Bed	2	6
Ditto, small ditto	2	0
THIRD FLOOR:—Bed Room	2	0

Large Apartments.

Large Drawing Room		
Ditto Bed. Ditto, with two Beds		
Small Ditto. Ditto, one Bed } per Day. 1	10	0
And two Servants' Bed Rooms		
Sitting Room Fire . per day	2	0
Bed Room ditto . per evening	1	0
Wax Lights . ,,	1	6
Breakfast, plain	1	6
Ditto, taken in Bed Room	2	0
Ditto, with Meat or Eggs	2	0
Ditto, taken in Bed Room	2	6

Private Dinner.

Soup, Fish, Joint, Entrée, Sweet, and Vegetables	5	0
Fish, Joint, Entrée, Sweet, and Vegetables	4	0
Soup, Joint, Entrée, Sweet, and Vegetables	4	0
Soup, Joint, and Vegetable	3	0
Fish, Joint, and Vegetable	3	0

Coffee Room.

Joint and Vegetable	2	6
Chops and ditto	2	0
Steaks and ditto	2	0
Cold Meat	1	6
Basin Gravy Soup	1	0
„ Julienne	1	0
„ Ox Tail	1	0
„ Mock Turtle	1	0
„ Mulligatawny	1	0
„ Mutton Broth	1	0
Plate of Sandwiches	0	6
Cup of Coffee	0	6
Cup of Tea	0	6
Visitors' Servants' Meals, per Day, each	4	0

Baths.

Warm and Cold, from Fresh or Salt Water	2	0

WINES & SPIRITS OF SUPERIOR QUALITY.

Sundays (in spite of opposition), and little could be hoped for until the general establishment of the custom of holidays with pay.[8]

But for those with leisure and money the improvements in roads and carriages meant that travel became progressively easier, and the numbers of travellers increased in times of peace. During the eighteenth century, seekers for health began to find their way to the Riviera and to places like Lisbon. Men and women alike began to travel further afield in search of culture and relaxation. So popular did this become that English writers of guides protested that it was 'not absolutely necessary to go to France for an atmosphere, to Switzerland for a Spa, or to Italy for a landscape'.[9]

Dangers of travel

At the beginning of the nineteenth century many of the centuries-old hazards of travel remained. Dangers facing solitary horsemen, such as Dr Syntax, ranged from losing oneself through defaced signposts and encounters with highway robbers, to the hardly lesser evils of country inns and the strengths of unknown local beers. A common factor in a guide book to England, as to the Continent, was advice on how to avoid some of the hazards. The traveller was subject to robbery, pilfering by pickpockets, or having the luggage cut off his carriage. In strange places there were mock auctions at which he might be tempted to buy plated goods for silver. He might be assaulted in the streets, or given false information. 'Advertising doctors' were special objects of caution, and in cases of ill health the visitor was recommended to seek the aid of the 'regular faculty'. Itinerant vendors of fruit 'especially the Jews'[10] were, it was claimed, 'constantly in the habit of smashing, or ringing the ranges, viz. changing the money given them for bad'. To avoid travellers being overcharged, guides gave lists of prices and distances for the hire of hackney coaches, rates of chairmen, charges for conveying parcels, and the fares of watermen. They recommended that one should note

13. *The Original Bath Guide:* Queen Square

the number of a hackney coach before entering it, so that if it should prove unsatisfactory, either by being dirty or unsound, or through the lameness or decripitude of its horses, the driver should be summoned before a magistrate.

Those who left the safety of their homes seeking amusement faced the evils of gambling and the possibility of meeting at balls 'females of prepossessing appearance and doubtful character [for they are] the most dangerous company into which a young man can be introduced [resulting in] years of vice and misery'.[11] There were publications specialising in this kind of advice. *The Countryman's Guide to London; or Villainy Detected* (1780?) spoke of the capital as 'a large forest of wild beasts, where thousands range about at a venture, are equally savage and mutually destructive one of another. . . . It abounds with hurry and impertinence, scramblings and underminings, villainies, cheats, and impostures'. *The Stranger's Guide, or Frauds of London Detected* (1808), began with a lurid frontispiece of a prostitute and her bully plundering a client. On the other hand, the antiquary and topographer John Britton (1771–

1857), in the twenty-fourth edition of *Picture of London* (which he revised as *The Original Picture of London* for a fee of 100 guineas in 1826)[12] aimed at 'recording truth, making impartial and disinterested statements, and leading the reflecting stranger to just, honest, and discriminating results'. He dismissed the tradition of cautioning travellers, telling his readers to use their common sense and avoid the obvious places of danger. Nevertheless his distinguished example did not prevent William Kidd from completing his *London Directory and Amusement Guide* (1837) with *London and All Its Dangers* and *London and All Its Miseries*.

Kidd may have been on uncertain ground when he estimated that 200 females were seduced in London each day (and more at the time of fairs). The report of the Royal Commission on Constabulary Force, 1839, certainly regarded highway robbery as virtually extinct throughout the country, and the turnpiked roads were credited with the improvement. To what extent crime had diminished and the safety of travellers increased was much disputed. Edwin Chadwick said there was a general belief that crime in the metropolis had been steadily increasing since before 1815 but that there was no evidence for this view. It is difficult to reach any firm conclusion.[13]

The problem of travelling by horse can be illustrated by the choice of vocabulary offered to users of guide books abroad. In, for example, Murray's *Handbook for Travellers in Portugal* (1855) the largest single topic, covering three pages, was that concerning the use and management of horses. A few of the phrases thought useful are:

Tell him I won't have the same horse.
I must have a better.
He is lazy, — hard in the mouth.
— kicks, — shies, — rears, — stumbles, — limps.
He goes down with one of his fore feet.
He won't go.

He does not walk well.
He is a tricky horse.

Even under the most favourable circumstances travel by horse was difficult, as can be seen from the diary of the young Princess Victoria on the quasi-royal progresses that so irritated her uncle, William IV. On 1 August 1832 the princess and her mother, the Duchess of Kent, left Kensington Palace at 7.06 am and changed horses five times before reaching Towcester, some 60 miles away, at 1.30 pm for lunch.[14] Such a means of travel was expensive, and providing relays of horses, which was necessary if one was to make any speed, demanded a high level of organisation. Society in the world of *Emma*, 1816, is fixed within a radius determined by horse power, and for John Knightley the relative merits of Cromer and Southend are settled by the ease with which he can transport children and servants and not by the advice of family physicians.

Most of the warnings related to travel on foot or using horses, but there were other means of travel open to those with money and stamina. For example, a centre such as Liverpool offered a comprehensive service of sailings to Ireland, a network on inland waterways and, from 1830, the Liverpool & Manchester Railway.

Modern progress

But improvements had been made. *The Manchester Guide* (1804) quoted with conscious superiority the claim made in 1754 for a Flying Coach to reach London in 4½ days. It comments: 'The mail

14. *Furby's Hand-book for Strangers Visiting Bridlington-Quay:* train

29

coaches now constantly travel that distance in thirty hours; and on the news of the late short-lived peace, the Defiance and the Telegraph coaches, came down in less than twenty hours!' The greatest change was yet to come, however. Thirty years later Dr Thomas Dick (1774–1857), a writer of popular scientific works, welcomed the new railway: 'The Liverpool and Manchester Rail-way, and the loco-motive powers of the machinery and engines which move along it, constitutes one of the most splendid and useful improvements of modern times. . . . Were this rail-way continued to London, it is calculated, that the journey from Liverpool to the metropolis, a distance of more than 200 miles, might be performed in eight or ten hours.'[15] He was not discouraged by the famous accident at the opening of the Liverpool & Manchester line, which caused the death of William Huskisson (1770–1830), the MP for Liverpool and a former Colonial Secretary.

Prince Albert used the railways from the early days of his marriage[16] but Queen Victoria did not take a train until the summer of 1842. She was delighted with the experience, finding this form of travelling not only much smoother but more private than road travel, when crowds gathered immediately her carriages even paused.

15. *The Picturesque Hand-book to Liverpool:* train and stagecoach

16. *The Picturesque Hand-book to Liverpool:* steam power

For many, however, the newest method of transport seemed hazardous and uncomfortable, even if the early prophecies of doom failed. There were others who shared Edward Parry's wonder:

Who would have thought that the steam which lifts the tea-kettle lid half an inch, could have been made the agent for propelling carriage containing hundreds of passengers at the rate of 60 or 70 miles an hour? and for driving huge vessels, carrying hundreds of tons and passengers, three thousand miles across the Atlantic in as many days as formerly took weeks?[17]

Changes in life
A reviewer of *Parry's Railway Companion* in *Archaeologia Cambrensis* for 1848 thought that Parry deserved high praise for putting into the service of archaeology 'that most unpoetic and innovating of modern inventions—the Railway'. The changes brought about by developments in modes of travel and their consequences were not always so

31

welcome. In *She Stoops to Conquer* (1773) old Mr Hardcastle had complained that the improved coach services brought into the country the vanities and follies of the town with disagreeable speed. Goldsmith's satirical comment had its earnest counterpart in the comment by John Britton that after the mail had begun to run along the Kendal and Shap road in 1786 there was a 'revolution in buildings, dress, furniture, food, manners and literature' such that local

17. *Walks Through London:* St Paul's Cathedral

EXPENDITURE.

	£	s.	D.
Parliamentary charges (£35,560 9s. 7d.)			
Expenses attending formation of Company and obtaining Act of Incorporation	20,000	15	10
Session 1845—Completion of line approaching Menai Straits	4,497	16	8
Session 1846—Proposed branch railways ...	5,007	0	7
„ 1847—Extension of line at Holyhead	5,254	16	6
„ 1848—Steam-boats	800	0	0
Land and construction (£2,895,603 0s. 2d.)			
Land and compensation	271,998	12	9
Works of roadway	1,691,904	16	2
Tubular girders for Conway and Menai bridges	424,725	11	8
Sleepers, rails, switches and turntables	295,474	16	0
Stations and approaches, water cranes, signal and mile posts.....................	70,285	2	10
Chester General Station...............	51,214	0	9
Incidental charges (£92,012 10s. 7d.)			
Land agency, £2,400; engineering, £53,689 5s. 8d.	56,089	5	8
Solicitors,—Land agreements, conveyancing, and general law charges...........	11,180	0	10
Direction and auditors...............	7,150	0	0
Resident director	4,101	9	8
Secretary and general office charges	8,428	3	8
Religious instruction fund	350	0	0
Advertising	1,175	9	10
Miscellaneous	3,538	0	11
Carrying Stock	1,368	12	0
Steam-boats	156,223	18	0
Interest paid to shareholders...........	124,755	14	10
Loans on debentures;—Stamps, commission, and interest	50,712	11	3
Dividend on preference shares:—25th Sept. 1848, at 4s. 1½d. per share	2,037	11	2
Working and other charges connected with traffic (ex: amount due to the London and North Western, for locomotive power and working stock; and ex: omnibus charges at the Menai):—			
Railroad—General working charges ...	8,767	6	9

K

Heads of Expenditure.	Amount of Cost to Completion.	Excess beyond Parliamentary Estimate.
Works of construction in excavations, permanent way, tunneling, masonry	£1,590,000	£254,000*
Stations	164,000	72,000†
Rails and Sleepers	286,500	95,000‡
Land	294,150	124,000§
Conway Bridge	150,000	50,000
Britannia Bridge	600,000	350,000‖
	£3,084,650	£945,000

Receipts and Expenditure to the 31st December, 1848.

RECEIPTS.	£	s.	D
On 42,000 £50 shares	2,044,467	10	0
On 42,000 £15 preference shares (5¼ per cent. per annum):—			
Deposit and calls on 36,860 shares, £15 each	550,635	0	0
Loans on debentures	682,994	7	9
Premium on shares, and interest	12,615	1	8
Transfer fees	494	12	6
Calls overpaid	475	0	0
Shrewsbury and Chester Railway Company (tolls into Chester), due previous to 1st May, 1848...	3,829	19	8
Traffic (ex: tolls due from Shrewsbury and Chester Company, and ex: earnings due 31st December, but not paid at that date to Company's account)	48,085	0	6
Loan at interest....................	75,000	0	0
	£3,418,596	12	1

* Of this amount there is yet to be expended, in excavations and finishing line between Bangor and Britannia Bridge, £25,000 and small works in Anglesea, the sum of £25,000

† Of this amount there is yet to be expended about 10,000

‡ The rails were calculated at £7 per ton; an average of £10 10s. has been paid.

§ Surplus land obliged to be purchased, about 400 acres more than Parliamentary estimate of 950 acres.

‖ Of this amount there is to be expended about 150,000

£185,000

characteristics were fast going into oblivion.[18] Access by tourists was facilitated by the road improvements, and new local enterprises grew up to meet the needs of visitors. Inns were built or expanded to cope with the new trade and ingenuity was used to amuse and entertain the newcomers.

These changes were recounted in the guides and possibly form one of their chief attractions for the modern reader. For example, *A Description of Brighthelston* [1780?] says: 'Most of the houses are built of flint stones, cemented with common mortar', and *Kidd's London Ambulator* describes Wandsworth as a 'pretty village in Surrey'. Houses may be destroyed by fire or other means, and such records as the description of Alton Towers preserved in William Adam's *The Gem of the Peak*, first published in 1838, become of special interest. The illustrations may record views long vanished or transformed. Descriptions of important works of art may be preserved

19.   *The New Illustrated Hand-book to Folkestone:* the Viaduct

in guides. Murray's guide to Oxford, 1860, is noted for its description of the frescoes at the Oxford Union begun in 1857 by Rossetti, Morris, Burne-Jones and others, which were completed by 1859 but became invisible within a few years. Maps and town plans record city centres since redeveloped. The relation between the guide and cultural change is therefore complex.

The impact of the new railways was even more dramatic than the coaching improvements.[19] New possibilities of travel were opened up, and a wide range of novel views of the landscape was presented by the new routes taken by the railways. The motorways today offer similar new views. In such towns as Stockport the railway made a dramatic and ruthless contribution to the skyline. Urban centres were renewed and provided with a succession of prestige buildings from which streamed scores of visitors (see illustrations 20 and 21). Railway time was gradually imposed and a whole new industry created, with its discipline and traditions. Old standard authorities had to retire: existing guide books had to be revised to chronicle this progress and specialist books (see illustration 46) written to assist the traveller cope with this new means of locomotion.[20]

20. *The Picturesque Hand-book to Liverpool:* Lime Street Station

35

21. *Chilcott's Descriptive History of Bristol:* Temple Meads Station

There was a great thirst for travel to satisfy; the average number of passengers carried weekly by the Leeds & Selby Railway during the summer of 1835, for example, was 3,500, compared with 400 previously carried by coaches on the same route.

As with the earlier improvements, so were these developments criticised. Wordsworth was not alone in his protest in 1844 against the intrusion of the railway and its effects on the environment. In his *A Guide Through the District of the Lakes in the North of England with a Description of the Scenery, etc., for the use of tourists and residents* he had already included a section on 'Changes, and rules of taste for preventing their bad effects' which recorded Gray's tribute to the Vale of Grasmere: 'Not a single red tile, no flaring gentleman's house or garden-wall, breaks in upon the repose of this little unsuspected paradise; but all is peace, rusticity, and happy poverty, in its neatest and most becoming attire.' Without sharing any romantic illusion about the happiness of poverty, Wordsworth's views on 'the primary sources of bad taste in rural imagery' have their modern expression, as also his praise 'of the beautiful forms of the ancient mansions of this country, and of the

22.   *Theakston's Guide to Scarborough:* train

happy manner in which they harmonise with the forms of nature'. He continues: 'Why cannot such be taken as a model, and modern internal convenience be confined within their external grace and dignity'.[21] This problem of reconciling the result of a tourist explosion with the conservation of what is the attraction remains unsolved, although all but a minority has ceased to become excited over the desecration of the Sabbath in the towns of Bowness and Ambleside and the dangers of tempting the humbler classes to leave their homes to the profit of pot and beer houses and the directors of railway companies. *Osborne's London and Birmingham Railway Guide* (1840), predicted 'great and material changes in society' but claimed that the 'mutual communication of facts and ideas' brought about by this increase in travel could only lead to an improved state of society.

23.   *Wallis's Brighton:* paddle steamer

CHAPTER TWO

Abroad

English travellers

Easier means of travel, even if these were far from the modern tourists' notions of comfort, brought out a less earnest traveller than those early determined seekers after classical antiquities and European civility.[1] The new connoisseur in the eighteenth century was interested in natural scenery, modern buildings and pictures. Naturally Italy was a chief centre of attraction, and guide books in French, German and English reflect the countries of origin of the new tourists. The English traveller might have used Thomas Martyn's *The Gentleman's Guide to His Tour Through Italy* (1787), which drew attention to pictures of special merit, or later Mariana Starke's *Information and Directions for Travellers on the Continent*, 6th ed (1828). This is packed full of practical advice on what to take, where to go, and how to get there safely. She goes into great detail, even to damning a particular hotel: 'Travellers . . . frequently experience bad treatment at Granvilliers; where the proprietor of the only tolerable inn the town can boast (l'Hôtel d'Angleterre), is neglectful and imposing'. For safety you might need a 'travelling chamber-lock', which could be fixed on any door in less than 5 minutes. She rewrote her *Letters from Italy* (1800) as *Travels on the Continent* (1820), and extended it to cover St Petersburg and to cope with such problems as hiring horses in Russia. For those in haste, she uses a system of exclamation marks to indicate items of special merit, following Martyn. This method is a precursor of the system of stars used by Murray and Baedeker, and even applied to English parish churches by Sir John Betjeman. Not all readers have been happy to accept this help. Aldous Huxley, in *Along the Road* (1925), cursed Baron Baedeker for sending him out of his way to see some dreary or nauseating picture. Recommendations like Baedeker's, however, are interesting in themselves for the light they shed on the history of taste, though they may cause surprise, as when Sir Henry Cole (as 'Felix Summerly' in *Pleasure Excursions: Reigate on the Brighton and South-Eastern Railways*, 1846) condemns 'Queen Anne's tasteless period'.

24. *A Topographical and Historical Guide to the Isle of Wight:* the Needles lighthouse

39

English guides

Apart from travel books, the English abroad at the beginning of the nineteenth century were well provided with a choice of guides. Samuel Leigh, bookseller and publisher of the Strand, who 'put an end to his existence by cutting his throat'[2] in 1831, advertised in 1818, 'Planta's *New Picture of Paris*, his *Gazetteer of France*, Vasi's *New Picture of Rome*, *The Belgian Traveller; or a complete guide through the United Netherlands*, Ebel's *Traveller's Guide Through Switzerland*, *A New Picture of Brussels and Its Environs* by J. B. Romberg, Schreiber's *Traveller's Guide Down the Rhine*, and *The Stranger's Guide to the Plains of Waterloo* together with maps, gazetteers, grammars, and tables of exchange'. Ten years later, in 1828, Baldwin and Cradock, the publishers of the 'Library of Useful Knowledge' for the Society for the Diffusion of Useful Knowledge, advertised 'Leigh's travelling books', a series of twenty-four volumes which extended to 'Reichard's Denmark, Sweden, Norway and Russia. 7s. bound' and 'Reichard's Spain and Portugal. 7s. bound'. Their other list of topographical books included four guides to Ireland—to Wicklow, the Giant's Causeway, the lakes of Killarney, and Dublin. A. H. Baily & Company, publishers of Cornhill, London, and Paris (through the Librairie des Étrangers), issued in the 1830s guides by Francis Coghlan to Brighton, Ramsgate, Margate, Dovor [sic], and a series of coast guides. Their list also included Switzerland, Belgium, the Rhine, the Netherlands, Hamburg, Paris, Calais, Boulogne, and a guide to St Petersburg and Moscow.

The firm of George Frederick Cruchley, the engraver, map-seller, publisher, and bookseller, was offering maps and guides to England, Wales, Scotland, Ireland, and a number of European countries in 1838. In another list about 2 years later he offered his customers a *Guide to the Levant* (9s), a *Handbook to the East* (15s), and a *Guide to Moscow* (8s 6d), together with many others. For those

MACASINS DE LA VILLE DE PARIS, 174 RUE MONTMARTRE

This magnificent Establishment, the most considerable in Paris, more particularly claims the notice of Strangers by its immense and various assortments of Lyons silks, Indian and French Cashmires, Laces, Mercery, its articles for Corbeilles de mariage and Trousseaux, and materials for useful and ornamental Hangings and Draperies for furniture

25. *Galignani's New Paris Guide:* large store

wishing to travel beyond Europe, *The Emigrant's Guide to New South Wales, Van Dieman's Land, Lower Canada, Upper Canada and New Brunswick* (1832) contained much information of a semi-official kind, and in the same year there was *Statistical Sketches of Upper Canada For the Use of Immigrants* and also *Practical Information to Emigrants including details, collected from the most authentic accounts relative to the soil, climate, natural productions, agriculture, etc. of the province of New Brunswick.* This suggests another type of customer. The first book in English published by the Free Press of Malta was Thomas Macgill's *A Hand Book or Guide for Strangers Visiting Malta* (1839). A major adventure was undertaken by those who explored fully the areas covered by John Osborne's *Guide to the West Indies, Madeira, Mexico, Northern South-America, etc. from documents supplied by the Royal Mail Steam Packet Company* (1846).

If the traveller crossed the English Channel without being properly equipped with a guide book, he could make good his lack of a suitable volume by calling in Paris on the firm of Galignani at the English, French, Italian, German and Spanish Library established for many years in the Rue Vienne and purchasing, for example, *Galignani's Traveller's Guide Through Holland and Belgium . . . compiled from the works of Boyce, Reichard, and Romberg.* The firm produced a daily English journal, *Galignani's Messenger*, and were the agents for, and sometimes pirates of, the works of the London publishing houses such as Bentley's Standard Novels.[3] In a cheaper guide,which gave lighthearted advice on smuggling and on cabinets, William Kidd the publisher said, 'At Galignani's you will meet your friends by dozens, if not scores—it being the general rendezvous for all the English'.[4]

John Murray III

If guides to England or guides in English to foreign parts are considered, one of the most famous names in the history of the genre, Murray, appeared late in an already crowded scene. John Murray III shared his motive for compiling and publishing the famous red handbooks with many other writers—dissatisfaction with the character and coverage of existing works. In an article in *Murray's Magazine* for November 1889 he explained how 60 years earlier he had brushed up his German and set out to tour Europe but found 'The only Guides deserving the name were: Ebel, for Switzerland; Boyce for Belgium; and Mrs Starke for Italy. Hers was a work of real utility, because . . . it contained much practical information gathered on the spot'. Murray also travelled with private notes provided by Dr Somerville, the husband of the eminent geographer Mary Somerville, but found himself in Hamburg without 'such

26.   *A Summer's Day at Hampton Court:* advertisement

friendly aid' and so began to collect information himself and record it in his notebook. His favourable view of Mariana Starke (1762?– 1838) did not last, for in September 1831 he wrote from Munich:

> I am sorry to find that Mrs Starke has been so precipitate in reprinting her book. The errors in the German part of it are innumerable, and I have taken great pains, ever since I first went abroad to collect information to improve it. A new and very much improved edition of Reichardt [sic] has recently been published. Would it be worth translating, do you think? The last edition, published by Leigh, is perfectly detestable—errors in almost every line.[5]

Mrs Starke's work which he was commenting on was first published by John Murray II in 1820 and had taken the form of a guide at the publisher's suggestion. This was not his earliest venture in the field of travel.[6]

The earliest of Murray's handbooks to the continent appeared in 1836 and included Holland, Belgium and North Germany; it was followed at short intervals by handbooks to Southern Germany (1837), Switzerland (1838),[7] and France (1843). These were written by John Murray III himself, assisted by friends, but as the series progressed, other distinguished, and sometimes eccentric, travellers and authors contributed. In 1850 Anthony Trollope, yet to achieve fame as a novelist, offered to write a handbook to Ireland. At Murray's request, he drafted some chapters, but his work was returned, unopened, 9 months later.

The fourth edition of Murray's *A Handbook for Travellers in Devon and Cornwall* (1859)[8] pays a quiet tribute to one of Murray's early contributers in the passage concerning Heavitree, near Exeter, 'the residence of the late Richard Ford, who here wrote his celebrated "Handbook for Spain". His gardens were adorned with Moorish

mine to the other by submarine passages descending on one side of the harbour and ascending on the other. Plans of the mines may be seen at the office in Lowther Street.

" One who has any feeling for the wonders of the old world, or any interest in the power of human skill, will do well to visit the Whitehaven coalfield. The enormous underground excavations, the costly machinery, the living world many hundred feet below the surface of the earth, the streams of gas perpetually rising from the coal-beds, the great breaks and contortions of the solid strata, the prodigious influence the mineral treasures are exercising over the whole civilized world, are assuredly subjects of no common interest, considered either physically or morally."—*Sedgwick* (see Introduction.) These mines are the property of the Earl of Lonsdale, and are worked by agents on his behalf.

The Wellington Pit and William Pit are the two great mines which chiefly support the coal trade of Whitehaven. The mechanical contrivances for economising labour and effecting the transport of the coal to the ships are admirable. The William Pit was (1864) raising 400 tons of coal every 24 hours, and 50 horses were kept permanently underground, some of them not having seen daylight for 20 years. The Wellington Pit is a mine of even greater importance, and the workings are deeper in consequence of the dip of the strata being to the S.W., making a difference of nearly 50 fathoms in the relative depth of the 2 mines. A temporary suspension of the working of the Wellington Pit took place in 1863 in consequence of the lowest seam (13 ft. thick) having been accidentally ignited by the fire from a stationary steam-engine employed underground instead of horse-power. It was found impossible to extinguish the flames except by letting the sea into the pit, for which purpose a

[*Westm. & Cumb.*]

boring was made near high-water mark, through which the water was permitted to flow for a week to the lowest levels, which, in 1864, had been under water for 12 months without any certainty that the fire had even in that time been completely extinguished.

The coal exported from Whitehaven in 1862 amounted to 196,294 tons, but in 1863 only to 151,583 tons ; the falling off having been occasioned by the diminished returns from the Wellington Pit from the accident referred to. The other great export from Whitehaven is iron-ore (hæmatite) from the neighbouring mines.

The great feature of Whitehaven is its Harbour and the noble West Pier, one of the finest structures of the kind in England. It extends 365 yards into the sea, is 57 ft. high and 60 ft. broad, and is built of sandstone obtained from the neighbouring quarries. It was designed by Sir John Rennie, and forms a fine promenade. The area of the harbour is 60 acres. The Castle is a plain mansion occasionally occupied by the Earl of Lonsdale. The churches are remarkable for nothing but their extreme ugliness. Paul Jones the notorious pirate landed here in 1778 with 30 men from an American privateer, and burnt 3 ships in the harbour. He had been apprenticed in the town in his youth, and fitted out a ship at Nantes expressly for the expedition. He was obliged to re-embark precipitately, but he took the precaution of first spiking the guns of the battery.

Conveyances. — *Steam-packets* to Liverpool, Belfast, Dublin, and the Isle of Man twice a week. *Rly.* to Workington, Cockermouth, Maryport, and Carlisle—trains 4 times a day ; and by the Furness Rly. to Drigg (for Wastwater), Broughton, Coniston, Furness Abbey, Ulverston, and Lancaster, 3 times a day.

c

terraces, and planted with pines and cypresses from the banks of the Xenil and Guadalquivir'. Although the first edition of Ford's book was unattractive in appearance and expensive (30s), it was an immediate success, selling 1389 copies in the first 3 months after publication. It has been described as 'among the best books of travel humour and history, social, literary, political and artistic, in the English language'.[9] Richard Ford (1796–1858) took his wife and family to the south of Spain in 1830 for the benefit of her health. Travel in Spain was both difficult and dangerous, but Ford penetrated into the most remote and inaccessible parts, where he consorted equally with grandees, bandits and smugglers. After his return to England he took 5 years to write the handbook. In a letter he wrote: 'I am sick of Handbook. . . . I am an ass for my pains. I have been throwing pearly articles into the trough of a road-book'. The scope of the work can be appreciated from the full title: *A Hand-book for Travellers in Spain and at Home. Describing the country and cities, the natives and their manners; the antiquities, religion, legends, fine arts, literature, sports and gastronomy: with notices on Spanish history.*

In marked contrast to Richard Ford was the author of *Murray's Handbook for Travellers in Portugal* (1855). Although his old nurse described him as 'the dearest, dirtiest, lyingest boy' she had ever known, her charge was the Rev John Mason Neale (1818–66), whose services to scholarship were recognised in the United States by Harvard University with the degree of DD, and in Russia by both the Tsar and the Metropolitan of Moscow. In England, in spite of his immense scholarship, his voluminous writings, his translations and his hymns (which are still sung), he received no high preferment in the church, but suffered persecution. He was one of the founders of the Cambridge Camden Society, afterwards known as the Ecclesiological Society, which marked him as an enthusiastic propagandist of the Gothic revival. He was also a devout member of the Anglican Catholic movement. Suffering from tuberculosis, he sought health by travelling. Debarred by episcopal prejudice from regular ecclesiastical offices, he was appointed to the wardenship of Sackville College, East Grinstead, and it was here that much of his greatest work was done. He has been described as 'perhaps the most brilliant and versatile priest of the Church of England in the nineteenth century',[10] but in his lifetime he was a highly controversial figure and was one of those who suffered indignities at the hands of Protestant mobs.[11] Neale's official income was insufficient and he had to write to support himself and his family.

The early volumes of Murray's series shared the characteristics of other guides with forthright comments (see illustration 27) but these were modified in later editions when a more impersonal style was evolved. The handbook on Switzerland is another example of how immensely successful they were. It went through eighteen editions (excluding the Galignani edition of 1839) between 1838 and 1891 for a sale of 45,000 copies. The second impressive tribute to their popularity is their recognition by the other great name in the second half of the nineteenth century, Karl Baedeker. His first *Handbook*, to Holland and Belgium, appeared in 1839, and in the preface he states that Murray's *Handbook for Travellers on the Continent* had formed its basis. His later works contain other acknowledgments to Murray.

In 1851 Murray published his guide to Devon and Cornwall as the first of the series devoted to England, Wales, Scotland and Ireland, and completed it in 1899 with the volume on Warwickshire. Prof J. Simmons says: 'These sixty volumes formed, collectively or individually, the standard equipment of the intelligent English traveller during the reigns of Queen Victoria and her son'. They also represent the English guide book in its developed and mature form. The success of Murray's series is not only a tribute to the quality of the books

A. "Iconastasis," or Screen for the Sacred Pictures.
B. "Bema," or Sanctuary.
C. C. "Soleas," or Choir.
D. Nave.
E. "Proaulion," or Porch.
F. F. F. F. Columns.

1. Principal altar.
2. Throne of the Archbishop, Metropolitan, or Patriarch of Moscow.
3. Side altar, dedicated to S. Demetrius of Thessalonica.
4. Side altar, dedicated to SS. Peter and Paul.
   These two side altars are separate pieces of the one chief altar ; but placed here to allow of access to them without passing through the Sanctuary.
5. Stairs leading to "the Chapel of the Blessed Virgin" in the cupola, where the election of the Patriarchs took place.
6. Stairs leading to the Sacristy, containing the relics and curiosities of the Church.
7. Tomb of S. Theognostus, } Metropolitans.
8. Tomb of S. Peter, }

a. a. a. a. Pictures of the Seven Councils.
b. b. b. Pictures of the Last Judgment.
c. c. c. c. c. c. Pictures of the Life and Death of the Virgin.
d. d. d. d. Pictures of the Patriarchs and Fathers of the Church.

9. Shrine, containing sacred relics.
10. Tomb of S. Philip, Metropolitan.
11. Sacred Picture of our Lady of Vladimir.
12. Tomb of S. Jonah, Metropolitan.
13. Tabernacle over " the Holy Tunic," presented to the Church by Philaret, Patriarch.
14. Tombs of SS. Photius and Cyprian.
15. The ancient throne of the Tsar (called " of Vladimir Monomachus ")
16. Throne of the Patriarch.
17. Throne of the Empress.
18. Place of the platform on which the Emperor is crowned.
19. Tomb of Philaret, Patriarch.
20. Tomb of Hermogenes, Patriarch.
21. Royal doors.
22. Platform in front of the choir.

The Pictures on the Altar Screen (A) *are thus arranged.*

1. The highest compartment, the Patriarchs ranged on each side of the Eternal Father.
2. The Prophets leaning towards the Virgin and Son.
3. Minute representations of the Life of the Saviour.
4. Angels and Apostles on each side of the Saviour.

5. The Sacred Pictures or Icons :
   (a) " The Blessed Virgin," brought by Vladimir from Kherson.
   (b) " The Saviour," sent by the Emperor Manuel.
   (c) " Repose of the Blessed Virgin," painted by Peter the Metropolitan.

On the Doors (" the Royal Doors," so called because the Tsar or Emperor passes through them on the day of his coronation) are painted the Four Evangelists, to represent that through this entrance come the Glad Tidings of the Eucharist. On each side of the Doors are represented (in ancient churches) Adam and the Penitent Thief, as the first fallen and the first redeemed. On the farther compartments are represented the Virgin and the Forerunner (the Baptist), and at the northern corner the Saint to whom the Church is dedicated.

On each side of the entrance to the Nave are (sometimes) represented the Publican and the Pharisee, as the two opposite types of worshippers. Where the Porch is extended, it contains the Pagan Philosophers and Poets, each with a scroll in his hand containing a sentence anticipatory of the Gospel.

The south side of the Church is always occupied by the Seven Councils ; the north side either by the life of the Patron Saint of the Church (in the Uspensky Church, of the Virgin) or by the Parables. In the Donskoi Church all the events of the Old and New Testaments are represented.

The Columns are painted with the figures of Martyrs.

28. *Handbook for Travellers in Russia, Poland, and Finland:* Plan of Cathedral of the Assumption, Moscow

PLAN OF THE PATRIARCHAL CATHEDRAL OF MOSCOW.

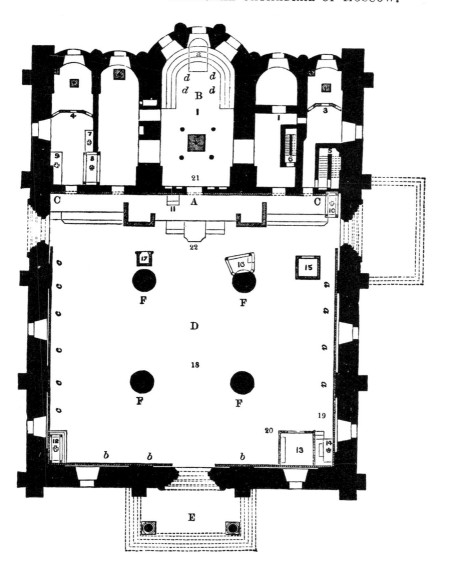

29.   *The Picturesque Hand-book to Liverpool:* paddle steamer

themselves, but an indication of the growing interest in travel and the thirst for information.[12] Murray's nearest rival was probably the Edinburgh firm of Adam & Charles Black.[13] Although Ward, Lock & Company had published the occasional topographical work, it was not until 1896 that they introduced their famous series, originally published in green paper boards; they later adopted the now familiar red covers.[14]

Foreign visitors
The number of foreign tourists in England was small but not undistinguished. The guides provided were few, and only in French or English. In 1654 Louis Coulon published in Paris his *Le Fidèle Conducteur pour le Voyage d'Angleterre* but gave few details. He found Westmorland a 'terre sterile et ingrate', but ultimately he did reach 'les isles dependantes d'Escosse'. A later seventeenth-century example is François Colsoni's *Le Guide de Londres* (1693).[15] These two guides may have been addressed to religious refugees as well as to travellers for pleasure. An early eighteenth-century example is the bilingual *Le Guide des Étrangers: ou le compagnon necessaire et instructif à l'étranger et au naturel du pays en faisant le tour des villes de Londres et de Westminstre*, published by Joseph Pote[16] in 1729. Pote, 'a very intelligent printer and bookseller', died in 1787 at the great age of eighty-four. He displayed his antiquarian interests

30. *The Windsor Guide:* Windsor Castle

in his own *History and Antiquities of Windsor Castle* (1749), which he abridged into *Les Délices de Windsore: or a pocket companion to Windsor Castle* in 1755, with five subsequent editions.

Le Guide des Étrangers contains a description of the two cities of London and Westminster and their modes of government, and a section on royal palaces, notable streets and public buildings, and the learned societies. There follow descriptions of the villages in the neighbourhood: Chelsea, Kensington, Richmond, Greenwich, Woolwich, Hampstead and so on. Then the guide goes a little further afield to Hampton Court, Windsor, Oxford, Cambridge, Blenheim, Newmarket, Epsom, Tunbridge, Bath and Bristol, commenting on antiquities and spas. There is a final brief section on the roads to Dover and Harwich and the costs of hiring transport. Although it has no maps or illustrations of any kind, it claims to be 'ouvre très utile et divertissant à l'étranger et au naturel du pays'.

Although the middle of the eighteenth century was to add seaside resorts and, later, the Lake district, Pote's choice of London, the universities, and the spas (especially Bath) remained the main

31. *Leigh's New Picture of London:* Plan of Hampton Court maze

subjects of the guide books for both natives and strangers. Visiting stately homes was a well established custom, which their owners had to take steps to regulate. Blenheim, for example, during the middle of the eighteenth century was opened on Sunday afternoons for 'persons of quality' at a minimum charge of 10s for parties of up to five persons. The Rev Dr William Fordyce Mavor (1758–1837), formerly writing master to the children of the Duke of Marlborough, set out the visiting hours in his *New Description of Blenheim . . . new and improved edition* (1793):

Blenheim may be seen every afternoon from three to five o'clock, except on Sundays and public holidays.

Company who arrive in the morning may take the ride of the Park before dinner, and after that visit the Palace, etc.

Shopping for Woodstock Gloves and polished Steel, both here unrivalled, may be attended to going or returning.

This edition advertises his *Nouvelle Description de Blenheim, le Palais Magnifique de Duc de Marlborough, dans la Province d'Oxford,* and some of his other works, most of which were for schools and some of which were translated also.

The presence of foreign tourists in Great Britain sometimes provided commentators with a useful literary tool with which to beat the locals. A 'native of Siberia' is introduced into *The Cambrian Tourist, or, Post-chaise Companion Through Wales*[17] and his exclamations on a visit to a chapel at Caernarvon for a service of the religious sect known as the Jumpers enforce the writer's own antipathy to 'enthusiasts'. 'On the commencement of the jumping, he entreated us to quit the congregation, exclaiming "Good God! I for a moment forgot I was in a Christian country. The dance of the Siberians, in the worship of the Lama, with their shouts and gesticulations, is not more horrid!" '

32.   *Chilcott's Descriptive History of Bristol:* quayside

CHAPTER THREE

At Home

Seeking the picturesque

A growing procession of intrepid Englishmen[1] and their families followed the example set by Celia Fiennes (1662–1741), who travelled between 1685 and 1697, and by Daniel Defoe (1661?–1731), who described his journeys in his *Tour Thro' the Whole Island of Great Britain* (1724–6). From the middle of the eighteenth century an increasing number of well educated middle-class tourists began to discover the fringes of Great Britain and fall under the charms of their native land. A key name is that of Thomas Pennant (1726–98), who published his *Tour in Scotland* in 1771 and *Tour in Wales* in 1778. There might have been one for Ireland, which he toured in 1754, but there he kept only an imperfect journal 'such was the conviviality of the country'. Later he travelled extensively in England and in Europe. With roads coming under the supervision of turnpike trusts and, at the end of the century, the virtual closure of Europe to peaceful travellers, together with changing tastes in landscape, journeys in the remoter parts of Britain became increasingly popular.

Travel here was still something of an adventure. Joseph Cradock (1742–1826), a Leicestershire man and patron of the London stage, wrote *Letters from Snowdon* (1770) and *An Account of Some of the Most Romantic Parts of North Wales* (1777). His party obtained a pony and a guide at Chester, and 'We set out . . . on our intended tour, and forming in our imaginations as many dangers and difficulties as Hannibal met in crossing the Alps'. This pleasant sensation of being something of a pioneer soon ceased and Mavor, who was constantly meeting other English visitors either singly or in groups, could say, in his *A Tour in Wales* (1806), that such travels were now 'the predominant fashion of the year'.[2]

The appearance of new centres of interest is important and reflects changes in taste. Literary influences also were at work. Scott's novel *Kenilworth* (1821), for example, popularised the castle and fed an interest already created by the romantic fiction of the period, so that a guide book can commend castle ruins as 'highly interesting. Here are all the horrors of romance and softer interests of novel might find a scene, and procure a local habitation. Cells built in the solid walls, dungeons impervious to the light of day . . . and all those incredients rendered so horribly relishing, by the works of Mrs Radcliffe, Monk Lewis, and their disciples'.[3] From Scott it quotes:

> If thou would'st view fair 'Kenilworth' right,
> Go visit it by the pale moonlight; . . .
> —home returning, softly swear,
> Was never scene so sad and fair.[4]

A Concise Guide to Kenilworth Castle, first published in 1777, ran into at least twenty-six editions by 1842 (the proceeds were to be devoted to the relief of the poor)—a testimony to the strength of the interest.[5]

The Lakers

The claims of areas of England once shunned were urged by those who sought to draw attention to the beauties of their own land and to

33. *The Oxford University and City Guide:* Mitre Inn

rebuke those who could only worship nature in her foreign shrines.
The attractions of the Lakes were firmly laid down:

> They appeal alike to the eye, the feelings, and the fancy; they teem
> with the varieties of majesty and loveliness. If they astound not
> with alpine masses clad in eternal snows, with fearful abysses which
> torture the shrinking vision, nor with great azure lakes, whose
> banks glitter with palaces, they present charms which affect
> the mind in a more harmonious and equally perduring manner:
> if they linger in the imagination less to electrify than to soothe,
> they achieve the great end of retrospection, which is rather a
> gentle passage of mild emotions than a series of abrupt and power-
> ful transitions.[6]

By the end of the eighteenth century the view of the Lake District
as a land of high, barren, and sometimes impassable hills of no great

56

use to man and little to beast had so far changed that, as in Wales, visitors had become tourists rather than explorers. It was possible to put them into a comic opera, *The Lakers*, in 1798.

> Each season there delighted myriad throng,
> To pass their time these charming scenes among:
> For pleasure, knowledge, many thither hie,
> For fashion some, and some—they know not why . . .[7]

But the guide book writers were on hand to instruct. The earliest of these was Father Thomas West (1717–79),[8] a Jesuit, who published his *Guide to the Lakes* in 1778. The book was reissued a year after his death in a revised and enlarged form, including an appendix of

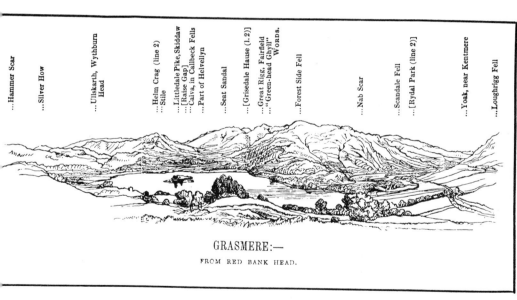

...Hammer Scar

...Silver How

...Ulskarth, Wythburn Head

...Helm Crag (line 2)

...Stile

...Littledale Pike, Skiddaw

[Raise Gap]

...Calva, in Callbeck Fells

...Part of Helvellyn

...Seat Sandal

...[Grisedale Hause (1.2)]

Great Rigg, Fairfield "Green-head Ghyll" WORDS.

...Forest Side Fell

...Nab Scar

...Scandale Fell

...[Rydal Park (line 2)]

...Yoak, near Kentmere

...Loughrigg Fell

GRASMERE:—

FROM RED BANK HEAD.

34. *A Descriptive Guide to the English Lakes:* Grasmere

over 100 pages which formed the most important anthology of pre-Wordsworthian writing on the Lakes. From this, rather than from the original sources, the majority of tourists found the views of Thomas Gray and others, among whom must be listed the Rev William Gilpin (1724–1804). Walters says of Gilpin: 'His is the quintessence of the Picturesque idiom; so much so that he was grotesquely parodied in William Combe's *Dr Syntax*, 1809'.[9] Taking Gilpin as his guide, West established the conventions for reacting to the English Lakes and provided a vocabulary in which to describe them. Armed with a landscape mirror or Claude glass, the visitor was directed to a series of stations from which to examine the scenery rather than to explore the area in general. Outlines of ready-made views were composed for the tourist and illustrated the guides. West describes the use of the glass:

> The mirror is of the greatest use in sunshine; and the person using it *ought always to turn his back to the object he views*. It should be suspended by the upper part of the case, and the landscape will then be seen in the glass, by holding it a little to the right or to the left (as the position of the parts to be viewed require) and the face screened from the sun. A glass of four inches, or four inches and a half diameter is a proper size.[10]

Changing tastes

Gilpin dismissed Snowdon as 'a bleak and dreary waste' that afforded little amusement to him, and such earlier travellers as Defoe and Celia Fiennes would have found the Lakers' enthusiasm incomprehensible. She is insensitive to natural beauty and only occasionally mentions antiquities. Her main interest is in human, especially economic, activities, and something of this view possibly survived in the traditional visit to the plumbago or black lead mine in Borrowdale. Certainly Defoe would have echoed the complaint of a writer in 1825 who noted the new reluctance to allow visitors to inspect workshops in Birmingham.[11] This interest persisted and is found, for example, in George Measom's series of official illustrated railway guides of the late 1850s and early 1860s, although some manufacturers continued to fear industrial espionage.

Plotting such changes in sensibility is a hazardous task. Four further illustrations may help to show radical differences in attitudes. As late as 1850, for example, the eighth edition of Jonathan Otley's *A Descriptive Guide to the English Lakes and Adjacent Mountains* told the visitor that the lunatic asylum on the moor outside Lancaster could be viewed by the curious with a ticket granted by the Visiting Magistrates. Secondly, in the year of Queen Victoria's coronation visitors to London were warned that '30,000 of the frail sisterhood are distributed through the Metropolis, offering as many temptations to sin as danced before the spirit of St. Anthony'.[12] By the 1860s

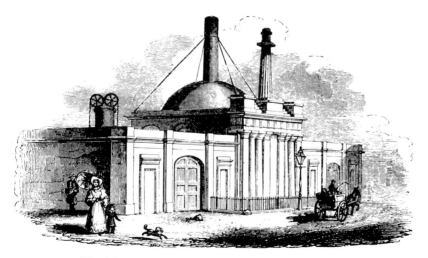

35. *The Picturesque Pocket Companion:* Margate gasometer

A

TOPOGRAPHICAL AND HISTORICAL GUIDE

TO THE

ISLE OF WIGHT,

CONTAINING

EVERY INFORMATION INTERESTING TO THE ANTIQUARIAN,
BOTANIST, GEOLOGIST, HISTORIAN, AND TOURIST ;

WITH

A BIOGRAPHICAL NOTICE OF EMINENT NATIVES;

REMARKS ON THE CLIMATE;

THE SANDROCK CHALYBEATE SPRING;

THE RATES OF PASSAGE, &c.

———◆———

TO WHICH IS ADDED,

A List of

THE MEMBERS OF THE ROYAL YACHT CLUB.

———◆———

By W. C. F. G. SHERIDAN.

———◆———

EMBELLISHED WITH A MAP, PLANS, VIEWS, &c.

———◆———

SECOND EDITION.

London :

PRINTED FOR M. A. LEIGH, 421, STRAND ;

SOLD BY THE BOOKSELLERS AT RYDE, COWES, YARMOUTH, AND
NEWPORT, ISLE OF WIGHT;

ALSO AT PORTSMOUTH, PORTSEA, GOSPORT, SOUTHAMPTON,
LYMINGTON, AND WINCHESTER.

———

MDCCCXXXIII.

36. *A Topographical and Historical Guide to the Isle of Wight:* title page

prostitutes cease to be mentioned in general guide books; they retreat into works specialising, from various angles, in low life. As a third example of changes in taste, the modern reader would hardly expect the gasworks to be included in the lists of public buildings to which special attention should be paid, but the original readers did not find this unusual; they took it as another encouraging sign of progress, set forth by the chaste classical designs of the facades of these buildings. Walking long distances for pleasure was considered highly eccentric until a change in attitude to 'pedestrianism' was brought about under the influence of Wordsworth, Coleridge, Thomas de Quincey (who achieved some notoriety for his *Confessions of an English Opium-Eater*) and others. It was popularised by George Borrow with his *Bible in Spain* and *Wild Wales*. In 1856 walking received the ultimate accolade when the Prince of Wales, then 14, was dispatched on a somewhat cheerless tour of Dorset with his tutor and an elderly colonel.

CHAPTER FOUR

The Guides

The English guide book

The earliest recorded use of the term 'guide-book' is in Lord Byron's poem *Don Juan* (1823), but the use of 'guide' to refer to a book rather than a courier is much older, as can be seen from titles already cited. *A Companion in . . ., The Stranger's Guide to . . ., The Picture of . . .* were fairly common ways of introducing a guide book. The originator of the term 'handbook' was John Murray II[1] and, following the success of the little red volumes, the word was adopted by such rivals as Nelson's in their *Hand-book for Tourists*[2] and, later in the century, Thomas Cook & Sons in *Tourist's* or *Traveller's Handbooks*[3] to European resorts and beyond. There were other and even lesser publications, but with no universal agreement over the hyphen.

It is easier to recognise a guide book than to define one, for the form has many variations. It falls between the extremes of a directory or inventory and a travel book, but shares certain features with them. The difference between a travel book and a guide has sometimes been likened to the distinction between the description of a meal and its recipe in a cookery book, but this is too neat. Guides are distinct from road books, but some, such as certain of the early railway guides,

ROAD SKETCH, No. 9.

JOURNEY from SHEFFIELD to MANCHESTER.

			Objects worthy of notice.
Little Sheffield -	1¼		Sheffield is the third market-town in the county of York in number of inhabitants, and celebrated for its hardware manufactures.
☞ to Worksop, 19½ m.			
to Huddersfield, 26¼ m.			
Barnsley, 13½ m. ☞			
Bents Green -	2	3¼	
Ringing-Low Turnpike	1¾	5	
☞ to Bakewell, 11½ m.			
Hathersage - -	4	9	Hathersage is a pleasant village, celebrated for the manufacture of needles and buttons.
Cross the river Derwent			Hathersage Hall is the seat of Ashton Ashton Shuttleworth, esq.
Hope - - -	4½	13½	L. Brough, formerly a Roman Station.
Castleton - -	1½	15	Hope is a small pleasant market-town.
☞ { to Tideswell / Buxton			Castleton, seated in a deep valley, is celebrated for its ancient castle and mines; the cavern; the shivering mountain, called Mam Tor; the beautiful fluor spar; the Speedwell level; the encampment on Mam Tor, &c. see History of, page 57.
Sparrow Pit - -	4	19	
Cross the Peak Forest Canal			
CHAPEL-EN-LE-FRITH - -	2	21	Chapel-en-le-Frith, a small market-town, see Road Sketch, No. 3. Near to Chapel-en-le-Frith is the celebrated Ebbing and Flowing well.
☞ to Buxton, 6 m.			L. Bank Hall, the seat of John Frith, esq.
Whaley Bridge -	3½	24½	Taxall Lodge, the seat of G. W. Newton, esq.
Cross the river Goyte and enter Cheshire			Lyme Park, the seat of Thomas Legh, esq.
Dishley - -	3¼	27¾	
Hoo Lane - -	1¾	29½	
Bullock Smithy -	1¾	31¼	
☞ to Macclesfield, 9¼ m.			
STOCKPORT -	2¾	34	Stockport is a large market-town, supported chiefly by the cotton trade.
to Barnsley, 33 m. ☞			
Huddersfield, 28m.			
Cross the river Mersey and enter Lancashire			
Heaton Norris -	1½	35½	Manchester is the second town in the kingdom in number of inhabitants, and is celebrated for its manufacture of cotton goods, in which the majority of the people is employed. It is the centre of a great manufacturing district: and by its close connexion with Liverpool, by means of the new rail-road, has become one of the most distinguished towns of the empire. It is the chief mart in the world for the articles manufactured in the surrounding populous towns.
Levensholme -	1¼	36¾	
Ardwick Green -	2	38¾	
☞ to Congleton, 23¾ m.			
Cross the Canal			
MANCHESTER	2	40¾	

37. *The Peak Guide:* road sketch

adopt a form derived from the road book, arranging material to suit the traveller as he goes along by pointing out the beauties and places of interest to the right and to the left. The early guides were fairly personal in their approach, and it was only after almost a century of experience of the form that the features associated later with Murray, Baedeker or Muirhead appear. These guides are impersonal, systematic, and designed for a single overriding purpose.

In general, guides provide short descriptive inventories of the places, institutions and monuments likely to be of interest to their users in the judgement of the author, whose personal feelings may emerge by implication or by direct comment. The provision of maps and plans, sometimes optional extras supplied at additional cost, further facilitate the stranger's progress. Later, illustrations and colour were added to make the books more attractive. To assist the traveller or to ease his stay information is given about transport and hotels, to which may be added details of postal services, local residents of note, solicitors, bankers, clergy, medical men and magistrates. To entertain him he will find information about theatres, libraries and excursions. Serious topics include details of church services, the state of local charities and the progress of education. To broaden the traveller's mind notices of local antiquities, customs, and lists of flora and fauna may be inserted, and, where necessary, notes of local dialect words commonly in use. All this and much more information must be digested and set down in a readable style in a book which can be read in the coach, or later the train, and kept in the pocket. As some of the most popular places had several guides, it was necessary to bring the information up to date regularly to keep pace with one's rivals, and some well established guides also stressed their longevity by claiming to be the 'original' guides.

Not all these elements are always present, and some guides change the form by concentrating on one aspect or another. George Kearsley's versions of Thomas Gray's *The Traveller's Companion, in a Tour*

38. *Kidd's New Guide to the "Lions" of London:* Covent Garden,
Theatre Royal

*Through England and Wales; containing a catalogue of the antiquities,
houses, parks, plantations, scenes, and situations in England and
Wales arranged according to the alphabetical order of the several
counties* (c1774), for instance, had grown out of notes written originally
on the blank pages of Kitchen's *English Atlas* during his tours
following the 'present prevailing passion for viewing and examining
the beautiful scenes which abound in our native country', and might
have been another book of travels. Its title is self-explanatory, and
its appearance in interleaved editions might be said almost to have
made it into a 'do-it-yourself' guide. An asterisk was placed against
entries for places of special merit.

Some publications cease to be guides with a map and become
introductions to a map and street directory. Is Thomas Cook's
*A Guide to Leicester, a list of streets, lanes, yards, etc., a directory of
the principal inhabitants, classification of trades and professions,
notices, historical and descriptive, of all the places of religious worship,
schools, hospitals, literary, scientific, benevolent, religious and political*

ON RIGHT FROM GLASGOW.	ELVANFOOT.—CARLISLE.	ON LEFT FROM GLASGOW.

ON RIGHT FROM GLASGOW.

Elvanfoot station.
The Lowther hills, 3150 feet high.
Glenochar.

Garshine.
Middlegill.

Rivax.
Auchen Castle.
Queensberry Hill, 2200 feet high.
Beatock station—for Moffat.
Kirkpatrick Juxta.
Lochwood Tower.
Rachills—J. J. H. Johnstone, Esq.
Wamphray station.
Johnston village.

Spedlin's Tower.
Dinwoodie—A. Maxwell
Nethercleuch station.
Jardine Hall—Sir W. Jardine, Bart
Applegarth village.
Viaduct over Dryfe Water

Lockerby station.
Lockerby village.
Castlemilk—Mrs. Hart.

Ecclefechan station.
Hoddam Castle—Admiral rpe.
Hoddam village.
Kirtle Bridge station.

Bonshaw Tower.
Beautiful scenery along the banks of the Kirtle Water.
Kirkpatrick station.
Branch to Annan and Dumfries.

Springfield village.
Gretna station.
Bridge over the river Sark, the boundary between England and Scotland.
Viaduct over the Esk river.

Rockcliff station.

Stainton village.
Viaduct over the river Eden.
Carlisle station.

ON LEFT FROM GLASGOW.

Elvanfoot station.
Newton.

Source of Clyde.

Howcleugh.
Raecleugh.

Greenhill.

Moffat village.

Beatock station—for Moffat.
Lochhouse Tower.
Poldean.
Viaduct over the Annan Water, 350 feet in length.

Wamphray station.
Oblique bridge over Wamphray Water.
Wamphray village.
Dalmakeddar.
Nethercleuch station
Millkbank—Wm. Roy.

Hillside—C. Stewart.

Lockerby station.

Bridge of 6 arches over the Milk Water. Fine view on both sides.

Ecclefechan station.
Viaduct over Main Water.
Bridge over the cross roads 120 feet in length.
Kirtle Bridge station.
Viaduct over Kirtle Water.
Elderbeck.

Kirkpatrick station.

Gretna station.
Skiddaw and Keswick range of mountains seen from this point.
Floristown village.

Rockcliff station.

Houghton House.

Carlisle station.

Mileage (from Carlisle / from Glasgow):
56 / 45 — Beltfield
54 / 47 — Newton, Lit. Clyde, Source of Clyde
39½ / 61½ — Beatock
34½ / 66½ — Wamphray
29 / 72 — Nethercleuch
26 / 75 — Lockerby
20 / 81 — Ecclefechan
17 / 84 — Kirtle Bridge
13 / 88 — Kirkpatrick
8½ / 92½ — Gretna
4 / 97 — Rockcliff
— / 101 — Carlisle

39.   *Black's Guide to England and Wales:* pages 502–3

ON RIGHT FROM EDIN.	From Berwick.	EDINBURGH TO DUNBAR.	From Edinr	ON LEFT FROM EDIN.
Edinr. station. Holyrood Palace, St Anthony's Chapel, and Arthur's Seat. Piershill barracks, with accommodation for 1000 cavalry.	58			**Edinr. station.** Waterloo Bridge. Jail and Calton Hill.
Portobello station.	55		3	Restalrig village. **Portobello station.** Portobello, much frequented by the inhabitants of Edinburgh for sea-bathing.
Musselburgh stat. A little to the right, Carberry Hill, where Queen Mary surrendered herself to the confederated Lords. Tranent, an ancient village, chiefly inhabited by colliers.	51½		6½	Inveresk church and village. **Musselburgh stat.** On Musselburgh Links the Edinburgh races are run. In their vicinity, the battle of Pinkie was fought in 1547. House where Col. Gardiner fell, and ruins of Preston tower.
Tranent station. Scene of the battle of Preston pans, where Prince Charles Stuart routed the forces of Sir John Cope in 1745.	47½		10½	**Tranent station.** Seton House, for many centuries the residence of the Setons, Earls of Wintoun.
Longniddry stat. Gladsmuir, the birth-place of George Heriot.	44½		13½	**Longniddry station.** Longniddry, interesting from its association with John Knox. Near the coast, is Gosford House, a mansion of the Earl of Wemyss.
Gullane station.	42½		15½	**Gullane station.** Balkencrieff, the property of Lord Elibank. From this Station, there are coaches for Aberlady and Gullane.
Haddington station. Haddington, the county town of East Lothian, distant seventeen miles from Edinburgh. On the south side of the town are the ruins of a Franciscan Church. John Knox is said to have been born in a house near the church. A mile to the south, is Lethington, a seat of Lord Blantyre's. Hailes Castle, (Sir J. Ferguson, Bart.,) was the chief residence of Queen Mary during her union with Bothwell.	40½		17½	**Drem station.** From which a coach runs to Dirleton and North Berwick, North Berwick Law and the Bass Rock, which rises 400 feet sheer out of the sea. It was long a stronghold of the Lauders. It is covered with sea-fowl of all kinds.
Linton station. Linton, a populous village, on the banks of the Tyne, which sweeps round its northern side, and falls into a large and deep linn. Nineware House, (James Hamilton, Esq.) Biel (Right Hon. Mr. Nisbet Hamilton) with its extensive plantations and charming walks. Belton Place, (Captain Hay, R.N.) Lochend House, (Sir John Warrender, Bart.)	34½		23½	**Linton station.** Phantassie, (T. M. Innes, Esq.) Tyninghame House, the mansion of the Earl of Haddington. Beltonford village. West Barns village. Beautiful village of Belhaven. **Dunbar station.** Half-way.
Dunbar station.	29		29	

67

40.   *Leigh's New Picture of England and Wales:* Doncaster grand stand

societies, municipal authorities, post offices, conveyances, by railways,
coaches, boats, waggons, and country carriers, to all parts of the
kingdom, with an almanac for 1843, county information, etc. to be
classified as a guide or a directory? The uncertainty is characteristic
of the formative period of the guide book; and so are the large
claims made in its title, which is a perfect substitute for a table of
contents (see illustrations 3 and 36).

Henry Besley, of the Directory Office in Exeter, published in
1845 (with subsequent editions in 1846, 1871 and 1877) *The Route*
Book of Devon: a guide for the stranger and tourist, to the towns,
watering places, and other interesting localities of this county: with
maps of the roads, county of Devon, and plans of Exeter, Plymouth,
Devonport, and Stonehouse. This illustrates how closely the guide,
with its maps and tables of distances, could come to the route book
and yet remain, with its continuous prose, a guide book. Many of its
concise entries suggest the style of a topographical dictionary, but
it is arranged geographically and not alphabetically. Editions of
Black's Guide to England and Wales containing plans of the principal
cities, charts, maps, and views and a list of hotels (first published in

We leave the Station at the Terminus of the Bristol and Exeter Railway, crossing the river Exe in a skew direction, by a wooden bridge. We then continue on a gradually rising embankment to the old Okehampton road, which is crossed by another bridge. We have on our left the ancient and prominent remains of the old city walls, and the numerous buildings that are thickly studded over the steep declivity that falls to the bank of the river Exe. On the right we pass in front of the St. Thomas' Union House, —the hills of Cleeve, and the grounds of Barley House, rising immediately behind it. From the bridge over the old Okehampton road, across Cowick-street, and on to the Alphington turnpike-gate the line is carried on a viaduct, a quarter of a mile in length, consisting of sixty-two arches, about twenty feet from the level of the ground. In Cowick-street is a Passengers' Station. We cross the Alphington turnpike road by a skew bridge, constructed of stone, a fine specimen of the skill of the talented engineer. We now proceed on an embankment gradually diminishing in height till it approaches within two or three feet of the ground. We here have a fine view of the south and western side of the city, with the noble cathedral, standing out boldly and above all the surrounding buildings—the vessels at the quay—and the high grounds on which Colleton Crescent stands, are all prominent objects. The country on our right becomes more open.—Haldon is seen in the distance; and the church and village of Alphington much nearer to us. We are now making our way on the right bank of the Exeter canal, which is here on our left, running parallel with, and a short distance from, the river. The precincts of Mount Radford, and the scattered houses and villas in the southern vicinity of the city, extending to the hamlet of Wear, are also seen at great advantage from this point. We are now opposite Countess Wear bridge. Here is a stationary engine house for exhausting the air from the tube. The town of Topsham is opening to view on the left, whilst on the right the wooded hills and mounds in the neighbourhood of Alphington, and the picturesque stone quarries of Exminster, with a few of the houses of the village, make their appearance. We pass in front, having a good view of the newly erected brick building

THE DEVON COUNTY PAUPER LUNATIC ASYLUM. The first stone of this extensive building was laid with masonic honours by Earl Fortescue, the lord lieutenant

ROUTE IX.

FROM EXETER TO DAWLISH, TEIGNMOUTH, TORQUAY, AND DARTMOUTH.

	Miles.	Furl.	Miles.	Furl.
From Exeter				
to Alphington	1	6	1	6
Exminster	2	2	4	0
Kenton	3	0	7	0
Starcross	2	4	9	4
Dawlish	3	0	12	4
Teignmouth	3	0	15	4
Torquay	8	0	23	7
Paignton	3	0	26	7
Brixham	7	4	33	7
Brixham Cross Gate	2	0	36	3
Dartmouth Floating Bridge	2	0	38	3

A TRIP ON THE SOUTH DEVON RAILWAY. We deem no apology necessary before entering upon our present Route by the usual turnpike road, in inviting the stranger to accompany us in a short excursion on this railway as far as Teignmouth, the point to which it is now working by locomotive engines.

Of all the beauties of scenery of which this county gives such an endless variety, and of which the numerous railways in other parts of the kingdom have opened to the eye of the tourist, there is none that can outvie in novelty and picturesque effect that which the present railway developes within fifteen or twenty miles of Exeter. The South Devon Railway commences at the Bristol and Exeter Station, and when completed, reaches Plymouth within the distance of fifty-two miles. It is to be worked on Samuda's atmospheric principle—a single line—with sidings at the stationary engines. Those engines are at intervals of about three miles. The atmospheric telegraph is to be laid along the whole line.

41. *The Route Book of Devon:* pages 170–71

1843) show how the route design developed for roads could be adapted easily to railways. Although there are plenty of passages of continuous prose, the close links between the forms are very notable. A copious index helped to interrelate the sections.

Another relation of the guide book was produced by George Bradshaw (1801–53), a Manchester Quaker, whose early business was as an engraver of maps and of plans of cities. In 1839 he began his famous series of guides to railways, and in 1847 introduced a Continental series. By 'guide' he meant, basically, a collection of timetables, but included maps and advertisements and such additional information as hackney coach fares. This is an extreme development of a very limited selection of data already found in guide books. The original idea has been claimed by another Manchester printer, John Gadsby.[4]

To amuse and inform

Many authors of guides and travel books knew that their work was for the entertainment and instruction of those who had no intention of deserting their own hearths. The stress on the lighter side of their function was such that some, such as George Kearsley,[5] went as far as to include the word 'entertaining' in their titles. Local permanent residents may have bought guide books for the historical information they contained, or for such features as tide tables, details of coach services, and carriers, and botanical or zoological data; or possibly to enjoy the advertisements, and certainly to relish the occasional critical comment; but the 'curious' visitor was the main audience addressed.

The Rev William Jenkins Rees (1772–1855), the Welsh antiquary, began his guide to Hereford, first published in 1806, by saying that 'the utility of Treatises of the nature of the present is so often experienced and acknowledged, that an apology for the publication of the work scarcely seems necessary; indeed, considerable surprise has been expressed by several, that Hereford has been so long without its GUIDE. To supply, therefore the deficiency, by furnishing the curious inquirer with a concise Account of the City and Neighbourhood, is the object of the present Publication'.[6] The Rev John Evans (died 1832), a schoolmaster, presbyterian minister, and the author of miscellaneous works, including several guides, claimed that 'the utility of books of local description is, at present, so generally acknowledged, that few places in the kingdom are destitute of some volume, which serves to direct the stranger to such objects as are considered, either curious or interesting'. His own book, *The Picture of Bristol* (1814), aimed to do this for Bristol, Clifton, the Hotwells, and their vicinity. Possibly many authors, while seeking to serve the public, also hoped to follow the example of Dr Syntax, whose record of his search for the picturesque was to make his fortune. The early readers of this once famous satirical poem on Gilpin probably did not appreciate the irony, for its author, William Combe, after squandering his fortune, was driven to various expedients to make a gentlemanly living as a writer, including supplying the textual matter to Ackerman's topographical publications.[7]

By the early years of Victoria's reign the number of tourists made it necessary to produce guides to most parts of England, its ports and market towns, spas and industrial centres. Although guides were generally based on centres of population and the surrounding areas, exceptions include the large group the Lakes[8] and those based on types of transport. A small number of occasional guides were inspired by special events, such as the Great Exhibition. Joseph Sturge, the younger, published the *Birmingham Saturday Half-holiday Guide* in 1871 (to reach a tenth edition in 1907), after the style of a London publication. It helped to make visits after midday delightful, with information on beetles, geology, fishing, cricket, fossils and railways.

The complex mixture created by the variety of readers' expectations, authors' motives and their presuppositions is a fascinating source for social historians of many interests[9] who are able to treat these guides with suitable discretion. For example, library historians will treat with caution the common statement in these books that the circulating library was *the* centre of fashion and jollity in the spas and sea bathing resorts, since these books were commonly written, printed, published and sold by the proprietors of the establishments whose social virtues they proclaim.

42. *The Hereford Guide:* County Gaol

Specialisation and decline

As the nineteenth century develops, writers become more aware of the guide's relation to other publications, and it surrenders its claim to comprehensiveness. By 1868 Black's *Guide to London* had relinquished some of its traditional fields and directed the reader to

Kelly's Post Office Directory, which may be seen in every hotel and in many shops, [it] contains the addresses of all persons in business as well as those of independent means. Webster's Red Book only gives the addresses of the latter when having houses of their own. Kelly's Directory[10] also contains a great mass of information as to persons in government offices, the conveyances and post offices throughout the kingdom, etc. Bradshaw's Railway Guide, published monthly, gives every information about trains and fares.

This process can be seen at work in the various editions of Harriet Martineau's guide to the Lake District. Certain publishers of guides were also proprietors of directories and so had the ability, and possibly the interest, to maintain distinctive publications. An early example is *The New History, Survey and Description of the City and Suburbs of Bristol, or Complete Guide* (1794), published by William

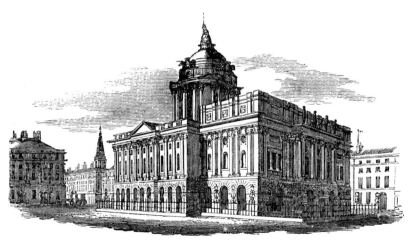

43. *The Stranger in Liverpool:* Town Hall

Matthews, who died in 1830 aged eighty-four. He was also the printer and publisher of *Matthews's New Bristol Directory, For the Year 1793–4*, which concluded optimistically by stating that 'The Bristol Directory is intended to be continued Annually, with Improvements'. In fact it did become 'one of the longest and most complete series of directories recorded'.[11] A later example is the firm of John Beck (died c1875) of Leamington Priors, which published fourteen editions of its *Leamington Guide* between 1840 and 1871, and from 1861 to 1897 an annual directory of the district.[12]

Among the descendants of the early guide books are today's dreary 'official' guides. These lack the personality of the author, discernible in the earlier publications, and avoid certain topics. The public relations officers of borough councils do not publicise lists of 'diseases and casualties this year' for example, or include sections in their guides warning visitors against swindlers. Early guides did not think a certain frankness on such topics incompatible with a highly developed sense of local patriotism.

Such a series as Methuen's *Little Guides* represents another aspect of the tradition, where the appearance of comprehensiveness is largely retained though the details have gone. They offer no advice on how to visit a prison, and no information on lunatic asylums, as do two earlier guides mentioned, and their lesser scope is not always viewed as an improvement. Prof Jack Simmons, commenting on the revised editions of the *Little Guides*, says that 'one cannot help feeling that the Victorians were saner and kept a better balance. Murray's Handbook of 1851 is still, from many points of view, the most profitable guide-book to use in Devon and Cornwall in 1951'.[13]

Guides to individual mansions appeared in the eighteenth century, A French edition of Dr Mavor's guide to Blenheim has been noted earlier. Other stately homes to have early guides include Burghley House, Chatsworth, Hampton Court, Holkham, Windsor Castle and Woburn. Cathedrals and churches such as Westminster Abbey

4½ *Boscastle* (*Inn:* Wellington Hotel). This little town is situated upon a steep hill, sloping to a valley, which at a short distance is joined by another, each coursed by a rapid stream, when they are together deflected towards the harbour and inlet of Boscastle. The, scenery in the neighbourhood is most romantic, and the country broken by deep furzy *bottoms*. Of the grandeur of the coast it is impossible to speak too highly. Boscastle has been so called from a baronial mansion, a residence of the Norman family of De Bottreaux, by which it was once dignified; and it still retains such names as Moise, Amy, Benoke, Gard, and Avery (? Yvery). It has a Valency brook, and a Palais and a Jardin. A green mound is the only mark of the castle of the De Bottreaux. In the reign of Henry VI. the heiress of the family was married to Robert Lord Hungerford; and as the possessions of that nobleman were situated at a distance of 100 miles in an easterly direction, it is probable that at this period the castle fell into decay. From the Hungerfords it descended to the Earls of Huntingdon, who retained it till the reign of Elizabeth, and whose heir in the female line, the Marquis of Hastings, is still Baron Bottreaux. The herald will remember the "3 toads" and the "griffin segreant," the arms of the Lords Bottreaux, in the ample quartering of the house of Hastings. The manor some years since came into the possession of the late T. R. Avery, Esq., who greatly improved the place and developed its trade, and it still belongs to this family.

The parish ch. of *Bottreaux*, or *Forrabury*, with its "silent tower," from which it is said the merry peal has never sounded, is situated above Boscastle, and close to the soaring headland of Willapark Point. It is dedicated to St. Simforian, who, according to the tradition, was buried in it, and hence, perhaps, the name Forrabury. An ancient granite cross, resting upon a pedestal of limestone, stands outside the churchyard. The following legend is connected with the church. Upon its erection, the inhabitants, long envious of the musical bells of Tintagel, determined to have a peal of their own. Lord de Bottreaux, then residing at his castle, aided the project, and a celebrated founder in London was directed to cast the bells. They were despatched by sea. The vessel freighted with them arrived safely off Boscastle, when the bells of Tintagel were swinging with sullen roar. The sound boomed over the waves to the ear of the pilot, who, elated by the welcome of his native village, piously thanked God that he should be ashore that evening. "Thank the ship and the canvas," exclaimed the captain; "thank God ashore." "Nay," said the pilot, "we should thank God at sea as well as on land." "Not so," quoth the captain; "thank yourself and a fair wind." The pilot rejoined; the captain, after the manner of captains, grew choleric, swore, and blasphemed. The ship meanwhile had closed the land, and the dark headland of Willapark and the precipices of the Black Pit were seen crowded by the inhabitants, eagerly expecting the precious freight. Suddenly a heavy bank of clouds, having gathered in the west, darkened the entire sky; a furious wind arose, and lashed the sea into mountainous billows. The vessel became unmanageable, and, driving towards the coast, capsized, and foundered, when all on board perished except the pilot, who alone, supported by a part of the wreck, was washed ashore, unhurt. The storm continued with extreme violence, and it is said that during the pauses of the gale the clang of the bells was distinctly heard, tolling from the ocean depths, and to this day the inhabitants recognise these solemn sounds during the also inspired individual guides. An early example is the *Brief Description of the Collegiate Church and Choir of St. Mary's in Warwick*, which was first published in 1757,[14] and again in 1763, 1775, 1790, 1793, 1820 and 1824, witnessing to the growing interest in local antiquities. The succession of guides to great houses and churches continues, and specialist architectural guides flourish.

Only a national institution may now be allowed to open his *Guide to English Parish Churches* with the words 'To atheists inadequately developed building sites . . .', but the incisive comments tucked away in the closely packed pages of Sir Nikolaus Pevsner's *Buildings of England* continue to demolish architects and upbraid civic vandals. Earlier writers could be equally forthright. Towards the end of a checkered career as printer, actor, singer, writer and composer, George Saville Carey (1743–1807) published his *The Balnea: or, an impartial description of all the popular watering places in England* (second edition 1799), 'the first work that gave a general account of those famed places of fashionable resort',[15] and it provides an example of the type of frank comment that is now missing from general guides. He says of Margate:

What the old Parade might have been is no easy matter to tell, but, in its present state, and in this improving age, it has little to boast of in respect of elegance, or even cleanliness, and in rainy weather it is a mere swamp; the greatest part of it lies between a noisy stableyard, well furnished with manure, and the common sewer of the contiguous market-place, as well as all the lower part of the old town, which frequently yield up the most ungrateful exhalations and unsavoury smells to those who choose to regale themselves in this delicious neighbourhood.

Possibly to indicate to visitors that Brighton at least was not indifferent to the problem of pollution, *Wallis's Brighton Townsman*

45. *The Manchester Guide:* plan

and Visitor's Directory (1826) published a 'Notice to house keepers' from the improvement commissioners on the movement of night soil and refuse.

Origins

With such variety of form and such a range of descendants, it is not surprising that the ancestry of the guide book is mixed. Esmond S. de Beer noted: 'The origins of the guide-book are to be sought in several classes of books'.[16] The first are works combining history and geography, such as William Camden's *Britannia* of 1586. These go back to classical antiquity, and influenced writers in the direction of impersonality. The antiquity of inventories of places is even older, for Joshua commanded the compilation of a survey which was to be registered on a scroll 'city by city' and brought to the camp in Shiloh.[17]

Road books and itineraries are more important, and, as already noted, influence the form of guide books. In Stephen Glover's *The Peak Guide* (1830), for example, they appear as a series of 'road sketches' in which the information about a journey between two towns is divided into three or more columns, listing the names of the places on the way, the distance between them, and notes or descriptions of 'objects worthy of notice' (see illustration 37). In England, the first real road book appeared in 1577 in the form of a chapter in Holinshed's *Chronicle*, 'Of our innes and thorowfares'. It gave an account of hostelries and inns, with warnings and observations, and set out a table of roads with distances in miles for each stage. A later attempt to deal with such matters methodically was undertaken by John Norden (1548–1626), whose *England, an Intended Guyde for English Travellers* was published in 1625 and gave forty plates of triangular distance tables. Ten years later appeared *A Direction for the English Traveller, by which he shall be enabled to coast about all England and Wales, and also to know how far any*

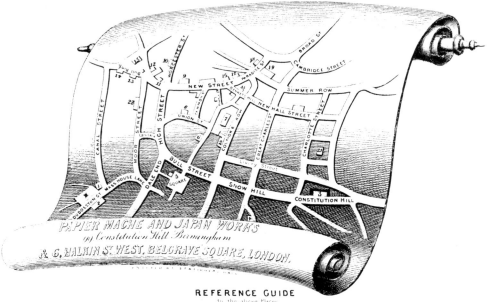

46. *Cornish's Stranger's Guide Through Birmingham:* advertisement,
Jennens and Bettridge's Works

market-town lieth from another. All travellers of the seventeenth and
eighteenth centuries owed their greatest debt to John Ogilby
(1600–76), who not only established the statute mile of 1,760 yd
(instead of the old British mile of 2,428 yd and various local measures)
but produced a road atlas in 1675 which provided the inspiration

79

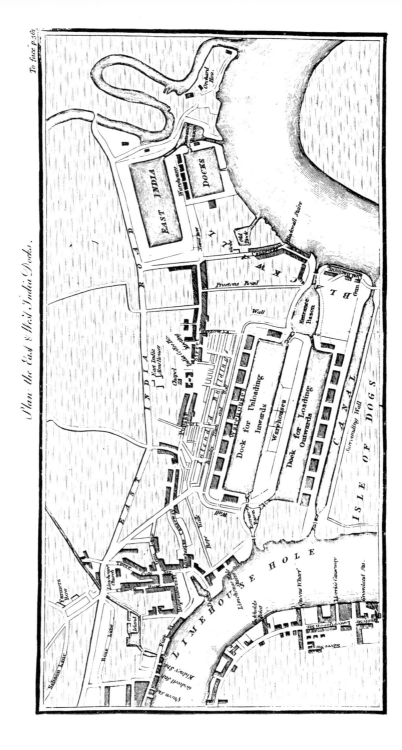

Plan: the East & West India Docks.

47. *The Picture of London, for 1810*: plan of the East and West India Docks

for future itineraries, and set a tradition which is associated with such names as John Cary (c1754–1835) and Daniel Paterson (1739–1825).

Maps

In general, eighteenth-century cartographers made little advance on the tradition of county atlases handed down by Saxton, Speed and Morden. Basically, they were still showing the relative positioning of places. Relief was illustrated with primitive molehill-like humps, and many of their connecting roads were still plotted conjecturally.

The period of the formation of the English guide book, roughly 1780 to 1870, coincided with the revitalising of cartography in England. The Ordnance Survey was established in 1791 and in 1801 produced the first of its 1in county maps, a series completed by 1867. Gradually the technically superior Ordnance Survey maps displaced unofficial maps of varying degrees of accuracy and skill, although some private map-makers, such as Greenwood, competed successfully for a time. Some guide book proprietors saw the advantage of the work of the Ordnance Survey and sought to use material from these maps in their own publications: for an example see *The Torquay Guide*, 3rd ed (1848) 'by several literary gentlemen', published and printed by Edward & George H. Croydon, the owners of news, reading, and billiard rooms at their Public Library in Teignmouth.

The guide books contain a largely unrecorded mass of material related to the main stream of British cartography. One of the most interesting groups consists of town plans, which are of varying degrees of completeness and ease of dating (see illustrations 45–7). On the undated maps such details as the presence or absence of railway lines may be used as clues to dating and, as with other material in the books, the printers, publishers and engravers should be sought in the contemporary trade directories.

CHAPTER FIVE

Readers and Guide Books

Social class

The amusements described in guides suggest a prosperous, but certainly not aristocratic, class of purchaser. The price for seeing the lions in the Tower of London[1] was 6d per person in company, 1s if alone; and the regalia 1s in company, 1s 6d singly, according to *An Historical Account of the Curiosities of London and Westminster* (1782). At Gloucester, Barrett's museum 'of natural and artificial curiosities' was thought to be good value 'at the easy expence of a shilling'.[2] Stately homes had housekeepers and gentlemen's servants who expected to be tipped by visitors. At Blenheim they were reported to be very attentive in extracting tips, and a visit to Chatsworth was generally thought to be expensive. The prices quoted in guides must be seen against the general level of incomes and of goods offered for sale in the advertisements or the notices of hotel keepers (see illustration 12). Men spinners in cotton factories, the 'aristocrats' of the trade, for example, rarely earned less than 20s a week in the first third of the nineteenth century, but in years of depression thousands might struggle to survive on much less. 'In 1842, probably the most distressed year of the whole nineteenth century, it was estimated that in Leeds at least twenty thousand people were living on incomes averaging only 11¼d. per week. Conditions were as bad in Manchester and in Sheffield.'[3] Interest in the poor rate and provisions made for the destitute or elderly are common features in even guide books written to amuse the visitor.

Hints on etiquette, and the reprinting of Beau Nash's rules for conduct from Bath, assume a certain degree of naivety or unsophistication in the guide book reader. Novices were advised on that still vexed question of tipping. *Black's Guide to England and Wales*, for example, in 1870 dealt with hotel charges and 'gratuities to servants' even before listing the contents of the book itself. Tips were graduated according to the marital status of the traveller and the length of his stay. So the advice is that 'A gentleman and his wife, occupying a sitting room and bed-room, 2s 6d. to 3s. 6d. per night for servants. If accompanied by sons or daughters, or other relatives, half this rate from each; but no charge for children under nine years of age'.

The social comments of the writers are also in keeping with the assumption of a genteel audience. At the seaside 'two women attend upon a lady when she bathes'[4] (see illustration 70). Leigh's *New Picture of London* (1818) says of the industrialised south bank of the Thames, 'this district is extremely unpleasant, if not unhealthy for human residence. It is therefore chiefly inhabited by workmen, labourers, and the lower classes of society'. In 1794 William Moss, a surgeon, in *The Liverpool Guide*, defended cellars as dwelling places for the poor in preference to the multiple occupation of houses, although the evils of this type of accommodation were already well recognised by his colleagues.[5] John Ryley,[6] in *The Leeds Guide* (1806), which he dedicated to William Wilberforce, eschewed 'knotty points of Antiquarian research', but explained that the rich selected certain parts of the town for their residence in order to avoid the columns of smoke driven eastwards by the prevailing winds. 'The water of the town is more contaminated by our manufactories than even the atmosphere . . .', he stated, though he did not explain how to escape from this evil.

A fairly high level of general education and wide cultural interests are presupposed by the authors. Classical allusions are used freely, but are generally not always translated. Whenever possible, an author assumed that his readers expected a fairly solid historical introduction. The quality of this varies from undisguised dependence upon existing standard works to concealed plagiarism of a single work, and to a claim to be based on the personal examination of original sources. The exact balance of historical and current material varied greatly. A large number of pages of *The Picture of Newcastle upon Tyne* (1812) are devoted to Roman antiquities, but a detailed interest is taken in the coal industry. The scholarly failings of a rival may be noted. For example, George Roberts, in *The History and Antiquities of Lyme Regis and Charmouth* (1834), wrote:

> The publishing, during the author's absence at a grammar-school, in 1817, of "A picture of Lyme Regis and environs", by a stranger who staid here two days only, which was necessarily meagre and unsatisfactory, forcibly recalled his attention to a history, which he commenced in 1823 making use of the materials which he could procure. He subsequently visited the Bodleian library, Oxford; the Tower; and the library of the British Museum on several occasions.

After considering the 'ancient state' of the town, a 'new etymology' is often proposed. Much of this material is no longer of value and is best appreciated in the early sections of, for example, Osbert Lancaster's satirical guide *Progress at Pelvis Bay* (1936).

John Britton dealt but briefly with the fabled origins of Bath and the more fanciful etymological excursions: he endeavoured 'to rescue truth from the meretricious trammels of fiction'.[7] Other authors of early guides shared this view, deprecating the padding of works 'by the recital of antiquated records, obsolete tenures, monumental inscriptions, and by long lists of perishing and perished names'. However, the unknown author of the *Leominster Guide* (1808) goes on to ask: 'What public avidity can the local historian kindle, who has no secret history to disclose, no mysterious policy to unravel, no heterogeneous coalition to analize, no dark conspiracy to bring to light, no dreadful revolution trampling upon ancient rights and immemorial usages, to trace to its hidden spring, and its remote consequences?' How indeed to interest the romantic reader? On the other hand, some thought it was possible to overdo the historical side at the cost of neglecting present beauties, or at least this was the excuse for publishing *A Guide to Weymouth* (1797?). The view that generally triumphed was that expressed by *The Gloucester New Guide* (1802) (published by Robert Raikes, printer and philanthropist) —'the reader will not expect to find all that an Antiquary would enquire'. It is endorsed by a reviewer of the third edition of *Description of York* in the *Gentleman's Magazine* for April 1816, who stated that the book had sufficient information for the inquirer and would induce further research in 'works of greater import'. Increasingly there were specialist guides, and so each author made his own estimation of the balance his readers required between information and amusement.

Some evidence about the original purchasers of guides is provided by the lists of subscribers occasionally found. Although a high percentage of people on the list will have been known to the author, of the 297 original subscribers to William Hutton's *History of Birmingham* (1782), which from its contents was virtually a guide, 244 are middle class, forty gentry and thirteen clergy.[8]

Some of the information contained in guides was of use to the

SHILLIBEER'S

PATENT FUNERAL CARRIAGE

COMBINES in one Vehicle, the necessary Funeral Cortege of a Hearse and Mourning Coach,—the Hearse part being so constructed as to contract and form seats for the Undertakers and Bearers to ride back.

This elegant Carriage is also particularly adapted for the

INTERMENT OF CHILDREN,

The contraction of the Hearse part rendering it suitable for any age, from the Child to the Adult, and totally distinct from the Coach in which the mourners ride.

TERMS:

	WITH ONE HORSE. £. s. d.	TWO HORSES. £. s. d.
Carriage in Town	0 10 6	1 1 0
Ditto under 4 miles..............	1 1 0	1 11 6
Ditto " 8 ditto	1 11 6	2 2 0
Ditto " 12 ditto		2 12 6
Ditto " 16 ditto		3 3 0

BLACK VELVET CANOPY FOR ADULTS, ⎫
BLACK & WHITE DITTO FOR CHILDREN, ⎬ EXTRA.
PLUMES FOR HORSES, IF REQUIRED, ⎭

ORDERS RECEIVED BY

Messrs. L'HERMITTE & BOYER, Bell, Hotel, Leicester ;

Messrs. G. & J. FOWLER, King's Head, Hotel, Loughborough;

Mr. CORDEN, London Road, or Mr. W. PEGG,
Black Head Hotel, Nottingham.

commercial classes. An early example is a pioneer guide to Bath and Bristol which first appeared in 1742. From the title of the third edition of 1755 the intended audience is clear: *The Bath and Bristol: or the Tradesman's and Traveller's Pocket Companion.*[9] Although it contains a succinct account of the origins and development of the two cities, forms of transport are its major concern, with details of carriers, wagons, coaches, boats and posts, tables of costs of sending letters and packets, and other matters of concern to traders. The enterprising printer of this guide was Thomas Boddely, the publisher of the first Bath newspaper, and seller of such commodities as 'Quicksilver Girdles for the Itch' and 'France's Female Strengthening Elixir'.

Prices

In view of the general level of wages, the cost of the earliest guides was high. *The New Oxford Guide: or, companion through the university* (1759), by, and definitely for, 'a gentleman of Oxford', cost 1s. *An Historical Account of the Curiosities in London and Westminster, in Three Parts* (1782) was 'Price Two Shillings and Six-pence bound', but it was possible to obtain the parts separately at a total cost of 2s. The fourth edition in 1823 of *The Student's Guide Through Lincoln's Inn* by Thomas Lane, the steward, must be considered rather expensive at 10s, although the engravings and limited prospect of sales may excuse this. The first edition of the popular *Guide to All the Watering and Sea-bathing Places* (1803) by John Feltham cost 12s in boards. Leigh's *New Picture of England and Wales* (1820), another fat little volume of national coverage, illustrations, and large map cost 13s bound. But these volumes with their hundreds of pages and many illustrations were exceptional. From Cruchley's *Catalogue of Maps, General and County Atlases, Hand Books and Guides for Travellers on the Continent, or Through England, Ireland and Scotland* of the early 1840s it is possible to make a wide

87

49.   *The Windsor Railway Companion:* advertisement

selection from 1s upwards. Prices over 10s are exceptional, and were usually charged for foreign guides or editions with extra illustrations, the latter being an important factor in determining prices. A copy of *The New Bath Guide* published in 1782 cost 1s, and some copies had a 'New plan of the city of Bath' which was priced 6d. A sixth edition of *The Northern Tourist's Guide to the Lakes of Cumberland, Westmorland, and Lancashire* (c1836) was advertised as 'Price 3s. with Six Engravings, by Westall, A.R.A. 5s. 6d.' Colour was also a factor: the Rev William Ford's *A Description of Scenery in the Lake District Intended as a Guide to Strangers*, 3rd ed (1843), cost 4s plain or 5s with the maps coloured. The bookseller and publisher of radical literature Abel Heywood published a series of *Penny Guides* during the 1860s in an attempt to appeal to a new audience.[10] This low price was made possible by the inclusion of an extensive collection of advertisements, and by vile printing. Less in bulk but more elegant were 'Felix Summerly's' *Pleasure Excursions*, sold generally at 1d and offprints from the *Railway Chronicle*. They were for excursions that combined a short journey by train with a ramble. A small but official *Popular Guide* to the Great Exhibition of 1851 cost 2d, and was aimed at a fairly humble level of visitor.

Between 1712 and 1853 advertisements were dutiable in varying amounts. Those in eighteenth-century guides generally advertise other books from the same publisher. Lists of patent medicines also appear. The custom of including such matter varied, but as the nineteenth century developed, advertisements became important and not the least interesting sections, generally placed at the beginning and end but sometimes intermingled with the text. The use of standard advertising matter for publishers' series is found later in the century. For example, there is *Black's Guide-book Advertiser*, which has its own pagination and sometimes a date more recent than that on the title page of the guide itself. Hotels and travellers' needs are commonly on offer, but schools and a whole range of commercial

50. *The Windsor Railway Companion:* tailor's advertisement

and industrial enterprises call attention to themselves. Such a guide
as *Cornish's Stranger's Guide Through Birmingham*, 9th ed (1855),
almost becomes an illustrated directory to the town's manufactories,
since over 400 firms appear. Some only give their name and trade, but
others take full pages and illustrate their factory and its products in
colour. The publishers list their agents in twenty-seven British and
twenty-five foreign towns in India, Australia, South America, etc.
Buyers of the guide received all this information in a feast of Victorian
typography, and 136 pages of text and illustrations of the antiquities
and current concerns of Birmingham for 1s.

In 1859 another 1s would have bought George Measom's *The
Official Illustrated Guide to the Lancaster and Carlisle, Edinburgh &
Glasgow, and Caledonian Railways, including descriptions of the most
important manufactories in the large Towns on the lines* (published
'under the authority of the Directors by W. H. Smith and Son')
and obtained 384 pages with 150 engravings, plus *The Official
Advertiser* with its 200 pages. Measom has sections on the commercial life of the towns, and his guides contain illustrations of the
interiors of factories and warehouses, and of machinery, either in the
text or in the advertisements, which form a delightful source of
information on Victorian social and economic life. The uncommercial
traveller, however, must have cursed the bulk of such volumes.
Measom was well aware of the value of advertising for street scenes
illustrated in his guides sometimes include a sandwich board man
advertising the guides themselves.

Bindings
A second edition of James Phippen's *Colbran's New Guide for
Tunbridge Wells . . . and Notices of the London and Dover Railway*
(c1844) was offered 'Richly Embellished and handsomely bound in
Cloth, 5s. An Abridged Edition at 1s 6d. Embellished with extra

Any of the following Articles may be had, Wholesale and Retail,

At W. SHEPPARD's
Royal Patent MEDICINE Warehouse,
Cpposite the *Post-Office*, BRISTOL.

BALM of Mecca
Steel Lozenges
Dalby's Carminative
Arquebusade Water
Black Currant Lozenges
Senate's Female Pills
Norris's Drops & James's Powders
Bateman's Drops
Essence of Mustard
Salts of Lemon
Brodum's Medicines
Solomon's ditto
Steers's Opodeldoc
Pomade Divine—British Oil
Godbold's Balsam
Balsam of Honey
Antipertussis—Grant's Drops
Solander's Tea—Sibly's Tincture
Iceland Liverwort
Dawson's Lozenges
Gilead ditto
Bath ditto
Marshall's Cerate
Velno's Syrup—Gowland's Lotion
Spilsbury's Drops
Hooper's Pills—Trowbridge dit.
Scotch Pills—Bath's ditto
Senate's Embrocation for Worms
Glass's Magnesia—Henry's ditto
Godfrey's Cordial
Ching's Worm Lozenges
Caracca Comfits
Daffy's Elixir—Squire's ditto
Hadfield's Tincture
De Velno's Pills
German Corn Salve
Issue Plasters
Huxham's Bark
Shaw's Ointment
Whittell's Black Drop
Cephalic Snuff

Bloom Cephalic ditto
Blair's Cephalic Fluid
Singleton's Ointment
Greenough's Tincture
Kreutzer's Tincture for the Teeth
———— Tooth Powder
Paraguay Tooth Powder
———————— Lotion
Wessell's Jesuit's Drops
Leake's Pills
Arnold's celebrated ditto
Hunter's ditto
Fleming's Liquid Blacking
———— Boot-Top Liquid
Nankeen Dye—Japan Ink
Huntley's Cushion Soles
Sicilian Bloom of Youth & Beauty
Seltzer and Soda Waters
Imperial Liquid Blacking, for
Ladies' Spanish Shoes
Furniture Liquid
Esprit de Rose
Lavender Water—Honey ditto
Cachou de Rose Lozenges
Cox's Medicines
———- Pearls
———- Essences
———- Fish Sauce Cases
———- Medicine Chests
Marking Ink of superior quality
Essence of Coltsfoot
Medicamentum, or Dutch Drops
Nailor's Corn Ointment
James's Analeptic Pills
Paregoric Lozenges
Coltsfoot ditto—Magnesia ditto
Refined Liquorice
Red Morocco Pocket-Books
Writing Papers, Pens, and Quills
Sealing-Wax and Wafers
Black-Lead Pencils

All kinds of FANCY WORK.

BOOKS of every description, in the most Elegant Bindings.

Engravings, bound in Cloth, 2s'. It introduces another variable in the prices—the bindings.

During the eighteenth century most books were given a temporary casing for distribution and then bound up to each purchaser's individual taste and pocket. Some booksellers would keep stocks available bound. James Lackington (1746–1815), keeper of a large bookshop which he called 'The Temple of the Muses', claimed in his *Memoirs* to sell 'one hundred thousand volumes, annually' and explained the difficulty of keeping each title in stock in a variety of bindings to suit the taste of individual customers. Some early guides survive in original boards, and a few have been bound up handsomely by their original owners, in spite of the fact that the useful life of such works is necessarily limited. Another problem on which Lackington commented as a result of his journeys in 1787 and 1790 was, that although he thought 'all ranks and degrees now read', the bookshops in the provinces had very poor stocks.

Possibly these or similar considerations drove the ingenious Sir Richard Phillips (1767–1840) to seek new retail outlets for his publications. Beginning life as an usher in a school at Chester, he was knighted when a sheriff of London, and enjoyed an adventurous career in various branches of publishing, including the production of a host of school textbooks under various clerical pseudonyms. Typical of his enterprising nature was his *Picture of London for 1802*, which was 'sold by all Booksellers and at all the bars of the principal inns and coffee houses. Price Five shillings, bound in red'. Innkeepers and proprietors of coffee houses were not going to be bothered with binding, so Phillips introduced a new type of roan binding and supplied his customers with books ready-bound. The rival publication, Samuel Leigh's *New Picture of London*, was bound in black basil.[11] Such sales were a development of an existing custom noted in Thomas Martyn's *The Gentleman's Guide in His Tour Through Italy* (1787), price 4s 6d half bound, which offered 'An improved Edition

52. *Cornish's Stranger's Guide Through Birmingham:* advertisement, Messenger and Sons

A

HISTORICAL DESCRIPTION

OF

WESTMINSTER ABBEY:

ITS

𝕸onuments and Curiosities.

LONDON:

PRINTED BY JAMES TRUSCOTT, NELSON SQUARE;

AND

SOLD BY THE VERGERS IN THE ABBEY.

1843.

53. *A Historical Description of Westminster Abbey:* title page

54.   *The New Illustrated Hand-book to Folkestone:* advertisement

of the Tour through France and Switzerland'; it was also published by Kearsley and sold 'at the principal inns at Calais and Boulogne'. William Penny, the proprietor of the Milton and Gravesend Circulating Library and Reading Room, sold his *Milton and Gravesend Guide* at the local bathing establishment and through stewards on board the steam packets, as well as making the traditional claim that it was sold 'by all booksellers'.

Penny retained the usual paper covers, on which was reprinted the title page with, usually, the addition of the price and an ornamental border. Over the next two decades the development of chromolithography enabled paper boards to be brightly decorated, an example being Henry Stock's *The New Illustrated Hand-book to Folkestone* (1848). Stock kept a library and a fancy repository, was an agent for teas and patent medicines, was a binder and picture framer, and advertised himself as a 'letter-press, copper-plate, and lithographic printer', Less enterprising publishers were content to use the services of such large commercial firms as John Leighton's, which, for example, provided a handsome cloth binding with gold and blind blocking for the fifth edition of *Theakston's Guide to Scarborough* (1854).

CHAPTER SIX

The Producers

Competition

It was necessary to make every concession to the convenience and interests of readers to survive in a very competitive market. In the early 1840s Cruchley was able to offer six guides to the Isle of Wight at prices ranging from 1s 6d to 10s 6d. In a town such as Oxford two guides, *The New Oxford Guide* and *A New Pocket Companion for Oxford*, competed between themselves and with other rivals during our period.[1] In Bath *The Original Bath Guide* and its predecessor held the field for many years.[2] In the Lakes competition was particularly fierce. Some guides, however, went through many editions and a few even survived into the present century, and it may be assumed their publishers thought of them as valuable properties. Possibly such considerations induced John Murray II[3] to pay Mrs Anna Brownell Jameson (1794–1860) £400 for the manuscript of her *Companion to the Public Picture Galleries of London* (1842), which included Hampton Court and Windsor in its coverage.

Survival depended on the business acumen of the publisher. The earliest guide to Southampton was published in 1768 by James

Linden, the proprietor of a circulating library, who started the radical *Hampshire Chronicle* 4 years later but went bankrupt in 1778 and thereafter concentrated his energies on a school he had helped to establish in 1773.[4] A rival librarian, Thomas Baker, began publishing his guide in 1774, and it ran through edition after edition for nearly three-quarters of a century, despite other competitors. Baker was also a bookseller, and later a dealer in Baltic timber, iron and hemp. He was at odds with the Corporation of Southampton over the petty customs of the port, and after the passing of the Harbour Act, 1803, became one of the commissioners responsible for the administration of the port.

The competition for customers made it necessary for guides to be as attractive as possible, with an increased number of illustrations and improved presentation of data. An outstanding example is the fifteenth edition of John Phillips's *Black's Picturesque Guide to the English Lakes* (1868), which has all the features of a guide of this period to this area, plus some illustrations by Myles Birket Foster, RA (1825–1899), engraved by Edmund Evans (1826–1905). It has also a superior binding to its rivals and to others in Black's series with an attractive green cloth cover gold-blocked by John Leighton, thereby combining several of the great names in Victorian book production (see illustration 66).

London publishers

Evidence of the commercial importance of guide books may be shown by the interest of a number of London publishing houses in provincial publications. The most important of these publishers was Longmans, who were the publishers of the later editions of *The Picture of London* (afterwards *The Original Picture of London*)[5] and *A Guide to All the Watering and Sea-bathing Places*, which had both belonged to Sir Richard Phillips. They were also one of the many firms appearing in the imprint of *The Ambulator; or, a Pocket*

Companion for the Tour of London and Its Environs, which went into many editions. Their provincial interests included guides to Fonthill Abbey and Woburn, to Cambridge, Ely, Hereford, Leamington, Leominster, the Isle of Wight, Newcastle upon Tyne, and the Lakes. Extensive links with the provincial, and indeed American colonial, trade had been established by the second Thomas Longman (1731–97), and by 1860 the house was described as the 'largest firm of book-merchants that this country has yet known'.[6] Not all their ventures in this field were successful. For example, a series on British cathedrals by John Britton, based on his larger works, was abandoned after the failure of the book on Norwich, the first to be published;[7] and attempts to reduce costs by stereotyping instead of resetting and updating each new edition of *The Original Picture of London* led to that work's ultimate supersession by its rivals.[8]

· Another important London firm was Baldwin, Cradock, & Joy, publishers for the Society for the Diffusion of Useful Knowledge and launchers of the *Westminster Review* in 1824. They issued guides to Birmingham, Hereford, the Wye, Devonport, and Woburn. Simpkin, Marshall & Company had interests in railway guides and guides to Harrogate, Henley on Thames, Ripon, Warwick, and, of course, the Lakes. William Sherwood (1776–1837), 'one of the oldest and most respectable publishers and booksellers of Paternoster row' who 'for eighteen years . . . never indulged himself with a holiday',[9] published such works as *Cyclopedia of Practical Medicine* and later *Cyclopedia of Surgery.* He had interests in several guides to the Isle of Wight, the Lakes, London, Brighton, and Arundel Castle. Whittaker & Company appears on the title pages of guides to Craven, Exeter, the Isle of Wight, and the Lakes. John Rivington's business in St Paul's Churchyard 'enjoyed the especial patronage of the clergy, particularly those of the higher order',[10] which was probably useful in promoting the sales of guides to Oxford, and later to such towns as Tunbridge Wells and, less obviously, Southport. William Lane of the

Minerva Press[11] in Leadenhall Street printed *The Hastings Guide*, 3rd ed (1804), and was one of the publishers of *The History of Cheltenham and Its Environs* (1803). His partner and successor, Anthony King Newman, published *An Historical Description of Westminster Abbey . . . Designed Chiefly as a Guide to Strangers* (1813).

Some guides were good commercial ventures. W. T. Moncrieff, for example, claimed that the first two editions of his guide to Leamington sold 3,000 copies when an edition usually ran only to 750 copies.[12] Many of the examples given above were fairly minor works with small sales, and it is difficult to see why major London firms should have been interested in them. Perhaps, as in the case of James Robson (1733–1806), one of the publishers of the early editions of West's guide to the Lakes, there was the link of personal interest in the area. Robson, the son of a yeoman, was born at Sebergham in Cumberland but made his fortune in the London book trade through publishing and book auctions, including the sale of the great Pinelli library.

The imprint of *The Cambridge Guide* (1830) illustrates the complicated arrangements for producing a guide and the participation of London publishers: 'Cambridge: Printed for J. and J. J. Deighton; Thomas Stevenson; and Richard Newby: and sold by Longman and Co.; C. J. G. and F. Rivington; Whittaker and Co.; and Simpkin and Marshall, London'. The book was printed by T. C. Newby, Angel Hill, Bury St Edmunds, who was also a bookseller, print and music seller and owner of a circulating library.[13]

Provincial publishing

Two other groups stand out among those who had a commercial interest in guide books: proprietors of circulating libraries and publishers of newspapers. In the state of the printing and publishing trades of the eighteenth and early nineteenth centuries these distinctions, which today indicate major divisions within the trade,

55. *The New Dover Guide:* advertisement

·

were largely meaningless, since there was a considerable measure of overlap. Even in London, printing was carried on as an ancillary to more lucrative trades (eg, by a rag merchant, an undertaker, and a manufacturer of pumps and water closets).[14] In the provinces also it was the exception rather than the rule to make a living by printing alone. Indeed, in the smaller towns printing must have been very much a side-line.[15] An examination of Warwickshire printers' notices, 1799 to 1866, lodged under the Seditious Societies Act of 1799, reveals thirty-eight occupations allied to printing. These were commonly bookselling, stationery, bookbinding or the vending of patent medicines, but included brewing and bacon dealing. Only a small number of larger firms was involved in book work on any scale.

James Drake of Birmingham, printing from 1825 to 1842, 'was the most prominent bookseller of his day and was connected with several magazines of a literary character'. He published a catalogue and offered special terms to schools and libraries. His work as a law stationer extended to abstracting titles and drafting conveyances, and acting as a commissioner for taking special bail. He printed forms, sold stamps and offered to obtain periodical publications. An early example of his printing is *The Picture of Birmingham* (1825), with textual matter by Hawkes Smith,[16] which was sold in London by Baldwin, Cradock & Joy. A particular attraction was its plan of the town centre in six colours (including white) to show the growth of the town from the time of Julius Caesar, a feat involving some historical imagination. This area of Birmingham has now been redeveloped more than once and all that survives of the pre-Victorian town is a few street names.

Newspaper proprietors
Guide book links with newspapers and periodicals varied: sometimes they were just printed on the same presses, and at others the news-

papers or periodicals acted as printers, editors and publishers. Richardson and Urquhart, 'under the Royal Exchange', were publishers of West's guide to the Lakes and also part-proprietors of the *Advertiser*, and Urquhart printed the *London Evening Post*.[17] The printer of *An Historical and Descriptive Guide to Scarborough and its Environs* (1787) was William Blanchard of York, who died in 1836 after spending nearly 60 years as proprietor of the *York Chronicle*. Richard Cruttwell, printer of editions of *The New Bath Guide* (1770–1801) was proprietor and editor of the *Bath Chronicle;* after his death in Cheltenham in 1793 he was remembered for 'A conscientious performance of his duty towards God, and an unbounded benevolence towards his fellow creatures'. He also printed 'the deservedly celebrated Bible of Bishop Wilson in 3 volumes 4to.',[18] which indicates a considerable business. Wood & Company of Bath, printers of the *Bath and Cheltenham Gazette*, printed *The Improved Cheltenham Guide . . . a new edition* (c1816), which advertised on its back covers that it was 'Sold at Heynes' (late Ruff's) Regent Library and Wine Vaults, Cheltenham'. Meyler's, another Bath firm, ran the *Bath Herald* and a circulating library, and were also responsible for *The Original Bath Guide*. This survived the firm, for an edition of 1919 was still published from the *Bath Herald* office when William Lewis & Son were the proprietors; and they proudly traced the origins of their guide through Meyler, and Richard Savage, back to Cruttwell.

William Meyler (1756–1821) was a magistrate and senior common councilman of the city, and had the reputation as a 'clever writer of small pieces of poetry'. Later Mary Meyler published Dr W. Falconer's *A Practical Dissertation on the Medicinal Effects of the Bath Waters*, Sir George Smith Gibbes' *A Treatise on the Bath Waters*, John G. Mansfield's *The Invalid's Companion to Bath*, and T. Mathews' *Advice to a Young Whist Player*. Her office, close to the Baths, was strategically placed for the sale of such publications, and also patent medicines. Samuel Gibbs of the Guardian Office printed and published *Gibbs' Bath Visitant; or new guide to Bath* (editions 1835 to 1866) whose selling point, in the early editions at least, was 'a plan of the city corrected to the present time, and engraved expressly for the work'. This suggests fierce competition, but the firms of Meyler and Cruttwell appear together in the imprint of *The History of Cheltenham . . . intended as a useful and amusing guide to the visitor and traveller,* printed by Ruff of Cheltenham in 1803. Thomas Kaye, who started *The Liverpool Courier* in 1807 and conducted it for more than 50 years, also published *The Stranger in Liverpool* (1809), which ran into many editions and is still one of the most interesting and well written of the guides to Liverpool, covering most aspects of the town. Although in his paper Kaye 'took strong party views, he was singularly mild and unobtrusive in his demeanour, and gained the regard both of friends and foes'.[19]

Librarians

The most important single group of promoters of guides were the proprietors of the commercial circulating libraries. A reviewer of

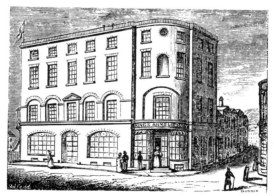

56. *The New Dover Guide:* the King's Arms Library

four rival guides to Worthing in the *Gentleman's Magazine* in 1818 was aware that 'Each Library has its separate "Guide".' These establishments varied considerably in size and importance and should not be confused with the more socially exclusive private subscription libraries.[20] The former type of library has been damned too frequently by Sir Anthony Absolute's description of it as 'that evergreen tree of diabolical knowledge' in *The Rivals* (1775). An analysis of library catalogues[21] shows that although many of them did purvey popular novels of the day to female readers, their stock included serious academic works in languages other than English on such subjects as history, philosophy, divinity, law, medicine, science, and topography. Just as it was generally not possible to make a living by printing alone, so few library enterprises were conducted in the manner we now assume to be suitable or even seemly. Commonly associated trades were printing, bookselling and binding; the sale of patent medicines, tea and trinkets; the hire of musical instruments and the promotion of concerts; less usually, the sale of coal and the keeping of 'select' billiard rooms or boarding houses;[22] and (though rarely) the issue of token coinage.[23]

The distinction is slight between the firm of Meyler's of Bath and the firm of W. Batcheller of the King's Arms Library (see illustrations 55 & 56) at Dover. G. B. Batcheller published *The Dover Telegraph and Cinque Ports General Advertiser*, a 'weekly family newspaper', from the same address. In 1828, two years after he established his library, William Batcheller printed and published his *A New History of Dover, and of Dover Castle, during the Roman, Saxon and Norman governments, with a short account of the Cinque ports compiled from ancient records, and continued to the present time . . . to which is added a new Dover guide, and a description of the villages near Dover*. It was priced 6s. This was an abridged version of a study he proposed to publish when he had the support of 300 subscribers. The scope of the stock of the King's Arms Library can be seen from the extensive

advertisements in his fifth edition of *The New Dover Guide* (1842).
On the title page he makes the not infrequent charge of plagiarism
against rivals in an unusually explicit form:

Large portions of this small work, first published in 1829, and
also of Batcheller's History of Dover, published in 1828, will be
found copied almost verbatim in Ireland's History of Kent,
published in 1830, and in Hunton's Watering Places, published in
1831. Without such a notice, and a reference to the dates, it would
be impossible to discover who were the real copyists.

57. *The Hastings Guide:* The Marine Library

58. *The Visitors' New Guide to the Spa of Leamington Priors:* Elliston's Library

W. Batcheller also published lithographic views of Dover, and was a letterpress and copperplate printer, binder, and bookseller whose stock included Harris's juvenile publications.

In addition to the examples already given, the following towns (with the names of the librarians) will illustrate the number of commercial circulating libraries publishing guide books: Brighton (Wright), Bristol (Prust), Buxton (Moore), Cheltenham (Bettison), Chester (Batenham), Folkestone (Stock), Hastings (Barry, see illustrations 4 and 57), Leamington (Elliston, see illustration 58), Leicester (Combe), Leominster (Burlton), London (Cawthorne),

Malvern (Southall), Manchester (Aston), Reading (Lovejoy), Scarborough (Coultas, Theakston), Southend (Renneson and Tarry), Tunbridge Wells (Colbran, Sprange), Weymouth (Bull of Bath), and York (Hargrove, also Bellerby and Sampson). In certain cases the librarian pioneered the publication of a guide and, if unable to print it himself, obtained the services of a firm in a town nearby or in London. An early example is *The Margate Guide* (1770), published by Joseph Hall[24] at his Circulating Library and Toy-shop under the New Assembly Room. His library was established by 1766 when he advertised in *The Kentish Post, or Canterbury Newsletter*, but he shared the publishing risk of his guide with Thomas Carnan & Francis Newbury of St Paul's Churchyard, London, whose firm and its successors are now chiefly remembered for juvenile publications. A guide with some of the finest illustrations is W. B. Noble's *A Guide to the Watering Places Between the Exe and the Dart*, published in 1817 by Croydon, printer and librarian in Teignmouth. The map was published 'by special Leave, from the Honourable Board of Ordnance'.[25]

Provincial printing

The extent to which the claims made by many provincial printers to be engravers and lithographers are valid can be tested, though care must be taken to avoid the traps of extra-illustrated editions, copies grangerised by their early owners or imperfect copies. Except for the earliest or simplest of the guides, printers generally needed some assistance in their production. Some examples will indicate the complexities. Although illustrations engraved by the firm of Neele & Son of the Strand, London, are to be found, it is their map work which seems to appear most frequently in guides, as in *The Picture of London for 1806* and *Leigh's New Picture of England and Wales* (1820) (see illustration 40). Their coloured map doubled the price of John Albin's *A Companion to the Isle of Wight*, 10th ed

(1828), printed by Mills, Jowett & Mills of Bolt Court, Fleet Street, London. Neele's provided a plan of the city for *A Guide Through the University of Cambridge* (1808), printed by M. Watson in Cambridge, and published in Cambridge by J. Deighton and in London by Longman, Hurst, Rees and Orme. Another of their plans appears in *The Cambridge Guide* (1830), printed by T. C. Newby of Bury St Edmunds.

The firm of E. Cave of York supplied maps for a number of local publications, such as *A Guide to Scarborough*, 7th ed (1832) which was printed by Mrs Jane Ainsworth, bookseller, stationer and librarian of Scarborough. Cave also contributed a map to John Richard Walbran's *A Guide to Ripon, Harrogate, Fountains Abbey, Bolton Priory, and several places of interest in their vicinity*, 5th ed (1851), printed in London by Bradbury & Evans but including lithographic work by W. Monkhouse of York. In *The Isle of Wight Visitor's Book*, 6th ed (1840), printed and published by Samuel Horsey, junior (a very indifferent bit of work, too), there is a map supplied by the London firm of Cruchley, successor to John Cary.

The work of a number of Edinburgh firms may be found, especially that of William Home Lizars (1788–1859), who in his earlier days exhibited paintings in Edinburgh but on his father's death was compelled to carry on the business of engraving and copperplate printing in order to support his mother and family. Examples of his work appear in several editions of the Rev William Ford's *A Description of Scenery in the Lake District*, printed by Charles Thurnam of Carlisle. He engraved the map for *A Companion to the Lakes* (1829) by Edward Baines, junior, which was prepared by Charles Fowler, surveyor of Leeds, and published by Wales & Baines of Liverpool. Another map of the same region but showing a development in his style is one Lizars engraved for the Ulveston printer and bookseller John Jackson, and it was used in Jackson's *A Complete and Descriptive Guide to the Lakes of Cumberland, Westmorland, and*

Lancashire (1847). Thomas Oliver, architect and surveyor, prepared a plan for his *The Topographical Conductor, or Descriptive Guide to Newcastle and Gateshead* (1851), which was engraved by Lizars, printed by R. Ward of Newcastle upon Tyne and published by the author. Further examples of Lizars' work are the illustrations for *Johnson's Historical, Topographical and Parochial Illustrated Guide and Visitor's Companion Through the Isle of Man*, 4th ed (1848), and the cover at least of William Howson's *An Illustrated Guide to the Curiosities of Craven* (1850), printed by J. Wildman of Settle, Yorkshire. Other Edinburgh firms whose maps were used include J. & G. Menzies, William Banks, and the great firm of J. Bartholomew, whose work will be found in many of Black's guides.

Minor examples of the work of well known firms of lithographers can also be found. London's first successful lithographer was Charles Joseph Hullmandel (1789–1850), who learnt the technique from Alois Senefelder, the developer of the process. Hullmandel made his own improvements[26] and 'did more than any other man to foster lithography in England'[27] and 'particularly the topographical lithograph'.[28] Examples of his work can be found in *A New Description of York*, 12th ed (1830), Mary Southall's *A Description of Malvern*, 2nd ed (1825), and W. T. Moncrieff's *The Visitor's New Guide to the Spa of Leamington Priors*, 3rd ed (1824). The last was printed by Elliston's British and Foreign Library at Leamington (see illustration 58), and has a view of Warwick Castle. The first real competition to Hullmandel came from the firm of Day & Haghe, successively lithographers to William IV and Queen Victoria; and examples of their work can be found in Robinson's *Guide to Richmond* [Yorkshire] (1833), printed by J. Wilson of Darlington, and in *Alderley Edge and Its Neighbours* (1843), printed by J. Swinnerton of Macclesfield. Work by John Brandard (1812–63), who specialised in music covers, appears in *An Historical and Descriptive Guide to Warwick Castle*, printed by Henry Thomas Cooke (1804–54) of

Warwick in 1838; it has a view of the castle which may be contrasted with that in Moncrieff's Leamington guide. Cooke printed and published other books on the antiquities of Warwickshire[29] and his guide to Warwick Castle ran to at least forty editions.

One of the very few guides that can be considered as an example of fine printing is *Ductor Vinogladiensis. Guide to the Town of Wimborne-Minster, Dorsetshire* (1830) by the Rev Peter Hall (1802–49). Hall edited Bishop Joseph Hall's works, as he claimed descent from the bishop, and was a bibliophile whose library, after his death, was dispersed by Sotheby's in 2,487 lots.[30] His scholarship extended to numerous theological works and editions of Bishop Lancelot Andrewes's *Preces Privatae Quotidianae, Greces et Latinae* (1828) and *The Private Devotions and Manual for the Sick* (1839). These, like the Wimborne guide, were published by William Pickering (1796–1854) and printed by Thomas Combe & Son of Leicester, whose printer's device was engraved by Orlando Jewitt (see illustration

59. *Ductor Vindogladiensis:* printer's device

60. *The New Bristol Guide:* Hot Wells

59). Fourteen copies[31] of the guide were printed on brown-tinted paper, and the general edition was well printed on good quality paper. The book is dedicated to John Britton, whose work did so much to popularise the study of English antiquities.

Illustrations

As the nineteenth century developed, the number of illustrations in guides increased and their quality improved. The earliest guides often had no maps or illustrations, and those they had were fairly crude. Some guides continued in this fashion, but in others great improvements were made. Sometimes the illustrations were inserted at the cost of the establishments depicted, as with the chapels in Batcheller's *The New Dover Guide*, 5th ed (1842). Librarians were fully aware of the value of illustrating their own establishments, either as an individual building or as part of a view. Improvements

113

in printing techniques and new developments played their part; examples have already been given of the use of lithography, and guides are also a storehouse of examples of engraving on steel, copper and wood.

In some of the examples given to illustrate the complex make-up

61. *A Descriptive Guide to the English Lakes:* Kirkby Lonsdale church and door

of these books, the work of one engraver, Thomas Orlando Sheldon Jewitt (1799–1869), occurs a number of times—in *A Guide to Scarborough*, 7th ed (1832), *A New Description of York*, 12th ed (1830), *Alderley Edge and Its Neighbours* (1843) and Walbran's *A Guide to Ripon . . .*, 5th ed (1851). Jewitt was an enthusiastic naturalist and illustrated botanical publications, but it is as an illustrator of works on archaeology and architecture that he is remembered (see illustrations 1, 59, 61 and 62). 'Jewitt's art was once widely appreciated: it opened the eyes of Englishmen to the beauty of mediaeval buildings and helped learned writers and leading architects to spread a taste for Gothic.'[32] His name or his monogram must have been familiar to the generations of students using John Henry Parker's *A Concise Glossary of Terms Used in Grecian, Roman, Italian and Gothic Architecture*. His wood engravings were introduced into the seventh edition of Jonathan Otley's *A Descriptive Guide to the English Lakes* (1844). They were also used in *The Churches of Scarborough, Filey, and the Neighbourhood* (1848) by the Rev George Ayliff Poole (1809–83), a strong high churchman and noted advocate of the revival of Gothic in numerous publications, and John West Hugall, church architect in the West Riding and secretary of the Yorkshire Architectural Society. Locally the guide was published by Theakston at his library in Scarborough; and in London it was printed and published by the firm of Joseph Masters, the publishers of *The Ecclesiologist* for the Ecclesiological (late Cambridge Camden) Society. Masters published other works by Poole, in addition to works by J. M. Neale, and F. A. Paley's *The Ecclesiologist's Guide to the Churches within a Circuit of Seven Miles round Cambridge* (1844). Jewitt, therefore, was contributing to a publication coming from the most orthodox circles of the Victorian Gothic revivalists. Parker's *A Handbook for Visitors to Oxford* (1847) is another work given distinction by Orlando Jewitt's engravings, which had been made for James Ingram's *Memorials of Oxford* (1837).[33]

62. *A Hand-book for Visitors to Oxford:* Provost's Lodgings, Worcester College

Jewitt's work also appears in Pugin's *Glossary of Ecclesiastical Ornament*, and illustrates articles in the *Archaeological Journal*. Indeed, to list all the works he illustrated would be to compile a bibliography of the major works in the antiquarian field in his lifetime.

Another artist/wood engraver of great charm was G. W. Bonner (see illustrations 9, 35, 39, 63, 64 and 65), who died in 1836. In 1835 Henry Vizettely was apprenticed to Bonner and later in his memoirs, *Glances Back Through Seventy Years* (1893), ungraciously dismissed his master as 'a second-rate wood-engraver'; but Bonner was also the master of W. J. Linton, who, in turn, taught Walter Crane. Many examples of Bonner's work can be found in the early publications of William Kidd (1803–67), and combined with the printing of C. Whittingham, junior, of the Chiswick Press, they give these guides considerable distinction (see illustration 65). Kidd's *New Guide to the 'Lions' of London* (1832) combined Bonner's architectural and humorous vignettes. A few were re-used as late as 1851 in *The Stranger's Guide in Brighton, for 1851*, but the paper and printing of this book fail to do them justice.

Possibly now as much an educational as an artistic curiosity is Sir Henry Cole's enthusiasm for promoting the employment of women to engrave on wood. He used them in his *A Hand-book for the Architecture, Tapestries, Paintings, Gardens, and Grounds, of Hampton Court* (1841) and *A Hand-book for the Architecture, Sculpture, Tombs, and Decorations of Westminster Abbey* (1842),[34] which he wrote under the pseudonym of Felix Summerly, His access to inventories preserved in the Public Records gave high standards to these guides, which, although unofficial, were 'sold by permission'. Cole is perhaps now best remembered for his suggestion of adhesive stamps, the 'invention' of the Christmas card (1843), as one of the organisers of the Great Exhibition of 1851, and as the driving force behind the building of the Albert Hall. Female wood engravers have endured less well.

63. *The Picturesque Pocket Companion:* Margate Market

64. *Picturesque Excursions:* Pegwell Bay

Illustrations in guides often pose problems. Some are identifiable as coming from other sources: for example, *A Guide to Peterborough Cathedral*, 2nd ed (1843) has a frontispiece taken from Winkles' *Architectural and Picturesque Illustrations of the Cathedral Churches of England and Wales.*[35] Other borrowings may only be suspected, and become the start of a piece of detection. An answer may be found in the activities of the Victorian remainder booksellers, such as H. G. Bohn, and the long-established custom of selling wood blocks and copperplates for re-use.[36]

65. *The Picturesque Pocket Companion:* device used by Kidd

CHAPTER SEVEN

The Authors

National names

Some authors of guides have been mentioned already. A few of their names remain in general circulation, though Wordsworth's is the only one of the first rank; his *A Guide Through the District of the*

66. *Black's Picturesque Guide to the English Lakes:* Wordsworth's home

Lakes was kept alive not on its literary merits alone[1] but by substantial additions, including a series of letters by the Rev Adam Sedgwick (1785–1873), who became Woodwardian Professor of Geology at Cambridge in 1818. Although Sedgwick published no single major book, and was always strongly opposed to Darwin's hypothesis as to the origin of species, he did important work and published a host of scientific papers. The mid-Victorian rival to this guide was *Black's Picturesque Guide to the English Lakes* by John Phillips (1800–74), professor of geology in King's College, London, and, later, keeper of the Ashmolean Museum, Oxford, from 1854 to 1870.

A poet laureate of a rather humbler reputation than Wordsworth, Thomas Warton (1728–1790), produced a skit on the Oxford guides called *A Companion to the Guide and a Guide to the Companion, being a complete supplement to all the accounts of Oxford hitherto published.* It was first produced about 1760, and as it survived in

67.   *The Oxford University and City Guide:* the Sheldonian

various editions into the nineteenth century, we can accept the description of it as 'a humourous production',[2] although the sparkle of most of its wit, its over-elaborate puns, and its learned jokes has dimmed with time.

Although his writings may not belong to the highest class of literature, many of the adventure stories written by Robert Michael Ballantyne (1825–94) remain in print and in circulation. He had been apprenticed as a clerk in the service of the Hudson Bay Fur Company and spent some time in trading with the Indians, but from 1848 to 1855 he was in Thomas Constable's Edinburgh firm of printers and publishers, and from 1855 wrote many novels for boys. *Ungava; a Tale of Esquimaux-land*, *The Young Fur-traders: a Tale of the Far North*, and *Hudson's Bay; or, Life in the Wilds of North America* may not be immediately recalled, but *Martin Rattler* and *The Coral Island* will certainly be familiar. These were originally published by Thomas Nelson & Sons and Ballantyne contributed a handbook to Edinburgh and also to the lakes of Killarney to his publisher's series of *Hand-books for Tourists*.[3]

Apart from these and one or two other writers, a list of authors of guides would now comprise only 'perished names'. Guides were often written anonymously, the authors hiding under 'by a lady' or some such description.[4] Others were by men of importance in their time and of consequence in provincial history, if not of permanent national fame. For example, the author of *A Companion to the Lakes of Cumberland, Westmorland and Lancashire* (1829) was Edward Baines, junior (1800–90), member of parliament for Leeds from 1859 to 1874 and editor of the *Leeds Mercury*, who was knighted in 1880.[5]

A small group of female writers of guides includes Harriet Martineau (1802–76), sister of the unitarian divine, and on her own account traveller and writer of a series of formidable articles and books on various social issues. Elizabeth Longford describes her as 'that dyspeptic Radical battle-axe'.[6] Her guide to the Lake District first appeared in 1855 but, aided by her niece Maria, it was much augmented in later editions.[7] A much earlier but lesser known female author was Sarah Aust (1744–1811), who wrote as 'The Hon. Mrs. Murray of Kensington'. Her *A Companion and Useful Guide to the Beauties of Scotland, to the Lakes . . .*, first published in 1799 and reaching a third edition by 1810, was written in a lively style and is an interesting source of information on the life of the peasantry.

Arthur Freeling was the author of *Picturesque Excursions* (1839) and a series of railway guides such as *Lacey's Railway Companion and Liverpool and Manchester Guide: describing all the scenery on and contiguous* [sic] *to the rail-way* (1835), *Freeling's Grand Junction Railway Companion to Liverpool, Manchester and Birmingham: and Liverpool, Manchester and Birmingham Guide* (1838). He also wrote *The Young Bride's Book: being hints for regulating the conduct of married women. With a few medical axioms* (1839) and *Flowers: their use and beauty* (1858). These titles suggest a hack writer ready to turn out a suitable text to meet current demands.

Another wide-ranging writer, of rather higher standing, was William Henry Davenport Adams (1828–91), journalist, translator, and author of some 140 works, including stories for boys and popular scientific books. In 1861 he produced *Black's Guide to the History, Antiquities and Topography of the County of Surrey* and in the following year *Nelson's Handbook of the Isle of Wight, Its History, Topography and Antiquities*. For a time Adams edited a newspaper on the Isle of Wight, but the link of a professional writer with his publishers was a more decisive factor in the production of this book that an interest in local antiquities.

Local worthies

Most of the guides were written by local enthusiasts, and their other publications are usually larger works on the same area or similar

68. *Beck's Leamington Guide:* Shakespeare's birthplace

guides to nearby towns or beauty spots. Their occupations range from gentlemen of means to impoverished tradesmen or failed school-masters. For example, John Preston, author of *The Picture of Yarmouth* (1819), was 'Controller of His Majesty's Customs at that Port'; and the author of *Sheridan's Topographical and Historical Guide to the Isle of Wight*, 2nd ed (1833) was the keeper of a boarding house (the establishment is given a good puff in the text and a large lithograph). Ebenezer Rhodes (1762–1839) was a master cutler but neglected his business in favour of editing the *Sheffield Independent* and publishing topographical works, including *Derbyshire Tourists Guide and Travelling Companion* (1837). The book gained him some reputation but involved him in financial loss, so that his business failed and before his death he became a bankrupt. The author of *A Descriptive and Historical Guide to Tynemouth* (1849) was William Sidney Gibson (1814–71), who began life as a journalist in Carlisle, but was called to the bar and became registrar of the Newcastle upon

69. *The Cambridge Guide:* view of King's College chapel

Tyne district court of bankruptcy. He became redundant after the Bankruptcy Act of 1869 abolished his and similar courts, to retire on a pension and devote his time to literary pursuits. Men like Gibson were enthusiasts and often entirely self-taught.

Two of the earliest guides to industrial and commercial centres came from local female worthies. In 1794 Jane Harvey (as 'By a young lady') wrote *A Sentimental Tour Through Newcastle;* and in 1804 Susanna Watts wrote *A Walk Through Leicester*, which was printed by T. Combe, a bookseller and proprietor of a circulating library. Susanna Watts (1768–1842) taught herself French and Italian and devoted herself to good works. Her own struggles against poverty and ill health created in her a deep sympathy for the sufferings of others, and about 1828 she founded, and helped to manage until 1840, a Leicester Society for the Relief of Indigent Old Age. Her guide is, as the title states, for a walk through the town and, although influenced by him, she was able to rebuke 'the elegant and

124

picturesque Gilpin' for what she considered his unsound views on a Roman tesselated pavement in Leicester.[8]

Medical practitioners

There are three other groups of authors of major importance in the field. The first is the medical group, whose specialist writings contributed so much to the success of spas and watering places and whose views and analyses of rival waters were quoted extensively by lay writers. The second and third groups are less clearly defined but consist of schoolmasters, local antiquaries and clergymen who devoted their leisure hours to scientific and historical investigations in their areas.

There are numerous major and minor treatises on the use of spa water by physicians of all grades of competence and repute. Two authors whose works survive with other than local or purely medical historical interest are Edwin Lee (died 1870) and Augustus Bozzi Granville, FRS (1783–1872). Lee, during a somewhat contentious career, divided his time between London and one or other of the watering places in England or on the Continent. He held the degree of MD of the University of Göttingen, and was elected a member of various foreign medical associations, including those of Paris,

70.   *Theakston's Guide to Scarborough:* sea bathing

125

Naples and Berlin. He published numerous works, several of which, on the use of mineral springs and on various spas in Germany, Switzerland and France, went into a number of editions. Beginning in 1848 with *The Baths and Watering Places of England*, he continued with books on Brighton (1850), the Undercliffe and Bournemouth (1856) and the southern watering places of Hastings, St Leonards, Dover and Tunbridge Wells (1856). His main interests were 'medical topography and remedial resources', and earnestly collected statistics of weather and analyses of waters. He admitted he had no great talent for topographical descriptions, so introduced into his works extracts from local guide books and standard publications.[9] His work was recognised by awards from the United States, Italy and France.

The second example, Dr Granville, had an adventurous career and was widely travelled in Europe and as a naval surgeon. His early interests included an enthusiastic participation in the politics of his native Italy and negotiations to secure the return of art treasures after the Napoleonic wars. He settled in England, but from 1840 to 1868 regularly spent 3 months of each year at Bad Kissingen, in Bavaria, whose repute he did much to establish. He published an account of his travels to St Petersburg in 1828, a number of works on public health issues and an autobiography. His writings on the merits of mineral waters include *The Spas of Germany* (1837) and *The Spas of England, and Principal Sea-bathing Places* (1841). He did not confine his remarks to purely medical matters but allowed his vigorous prejudices free rein. When describing Birmingham, for example, he attacks 'the Papists' as 'some of the earliest and most determined of the dissenters from the pure and primitive Apostolic Church of Christ'. At one stage he fancied he was travelling in a Roman Catholic country, so many signs of Popery did he find. At Birmingham he visited the cathedral church of St Chad, which had just been opened, and was informed that Mr Pugin was 'engaged in

Comparative Meteorology of Torquay and England generally.

	Mean Temperature.	Maximum Temperature.	Minimum Temperature.	Mean Daily Range.	Quarterly Range.	Days of Rain.	Inches of Rain.	Grains of vapour in cubic foot of Air.	Do. required to saturate do.	Mean Humidity.
	deg.	deg.	deg.	d·g	deg			deg		
Torquay	50·3	76	27	9·9	18	155	27·1	3·4	·9	·76
England	48·3	83	15	14·5	46	170	25·5	3·4	·7	·82

Quantity of Rain in inches.

	Annual.	Winter.	Spring.	Summer.	Autumn.
Torquay	28·20	6·82	5·61	6·38	9·39
Average of other places }	30·37	6·66	5·69	6·92	10·17
Difference in favour of Torquay }	2·17	·84	·03	·54	·78

"As compared with Clifton, which Dr. Chisholm describes as possessing 'an atmosphere elastic, vivifying, *not humid*,' and which Sir James Clark pronounces to be 'the driest climate in the West of England,' Torquay appears to great advantage. The following table is compiled from observations taken at the Bristol Institution and at Woodfield (Torquay), during the years 1842-3-4-5, and at Exeter, from 1832 to 1836, as given by Dr. Shapter, in his 'Climate of Devon':—

Torquay.

	Winter.	Spring.	Summer.	Autumn.	Annual.
Temperature	53·5	55·4	59·9	49·5	52·7
Dew-point	39·4	47·4	53·6	45·3	45·9
Difference	4·1	8·0	6·3	4·2	6·8

Bristol.

	Winter.	Spring.	Summer.	Autumn.	Annual.
Temperature	4·3	56·8	62·4	47·6	52·2
Dew-point	38·7	51·5	57·7	46·5	48·6
Difference	2·6	5·3	4·7	1·1	3·6

Average number of Days upon which Rain falls.

	Annual.	Winter.	Spring.	Summer.	Autumn.
Torquay	132	35	30	32	35
Cove	131	37	29	30	35
Penzance	178	50	40	39	48
Undercliff	146	39	32	33	42
Clifton	169	45	36	41	45
Exeter	162	42	36	41	41
Hastings	153	39	31	33	49
London	178	48	43	44	43
Sidmouth	141	40	33	32	35
Rome	117	35	30	17	34
Madeira	70	23	18	6	22

Quantity of Rain in inches.

	Annual.	Winter.	Spring.	Summer.	Autumn.
Torquay	28·20	6·82	5·61	6·38	9·39
Cove	33·25	10·54	4·05	7·05	11·92
Penzance	44·66	12·64	9·35	9·34	13·33
Undercliff	23·48	4·65	4·06	4·29	9·48
Clifton	32·56	8·43	5·69	9·44	9·00
Exeter	31·90	9·10	6·55	7·10	9·20
Hastings	32·81	7·59	5·80	6·40	13·02
London	24·80	5·85	4·80	6·67	7·43
Sidmouth	22·68	5·29	5·57	5·66	7·46
Nice	26·81	7·30	6·64	2·75	10·12
Rome	31·11	9·49	6·29	4·16	11·17
Madeira	29·23	11·40	5·77	1·45	10·61

Average number of Days upon which Rain falls.

	Annual.	Winter.	Spring.	Summer.	Autumn.
Torquay	132	35	30	32	35
Average of other places	160	43	36	37	43
Difference in favour of Torquay }	28	8	6	5	8

The following shows the general summary of the meteorology of Torquay and South Devon contrasted with the average of England:—

71. *The Watering Places of England:* rainfall statistics

superintending the construction of twenty-one other Roman catholic churches, principally in the Gothic or English style of architecture'. Going on, however, he praises St Mary's College, Oscott, the Catholic seminary, in spite of the views he had expressed earlier.

Some spas had their own medical guides, which were often written by local physicians and popularised serious scientific investigations into the use of the waters and their curative properties. Some were engagingly frank. To take two examples from Harrogate, Dr Adam Hunter, physician to the General Infirmary, House of Recovery, and Public Dispensary of Leeds, said:

> I shall not endeavour, as has been gravely attempted by some, to persuade any one that water loaded with sulphuretted and carburetted hydrogen gasses is pleasant to the taste; yet, however nauseous or disgusting at first, it is generally allowed that it becomes much less disagreeable by use. A bite of plain bread or biscuit will take off the fetor, and reconcile the palate as effectually and more harmlessly than any spice or aromatic, which is frequently used for this purpose.[10]

Alfred Smith, FRCS, surgeon to the Ripon Dispensary, for the second example, had some forthright remarks on hypochondriasis:

> In the nineteenth [century], we may venture to assert, that *nervous disorders* have taken the place of fevers, and may justly be reckoned two thirds of the whole with which civilized society is afflicted . . . nervous ailments are not now confined to the higher ranks, but are spreading rapidly with the extension of knowledge and luxury among the poorer classes.

He goes on to list possible causes and his suggestions include 'the anxieties of competition' and 'sedentary habits'. His most interesting case seemed to be 'a gentleman who entertained a firm conviction that he was a book; or, as he himself expressed it, "a work", and the only matter that perplexed him, and upon which he seriously asked my opinion was, "whether he was in one volume or two".'[11]

Antiquaries

Such personal dicta were not confined to physicians or surgeons. The authors of *The Churches of Scarborough, Filey, and the Neighbourhood* (1848) betray in almost every comment and description their adherence to a certain school of antiquarian and ecclesiological thought. Even their spelling of 'pues' (pews) evokes echoes of the fierce controversies on church matters during their period. Jonathan Otley, in his very popular *A Descriptive Guide to the English Lakes and Adjacent Mountains: with notices of the botany, mineralogy, and geology of the district*, can denounce the 'execrable taste of some modern Goths' for the 'barn-like appearance' of Kirkby Lonsdale church (see illustration 61): 'The same rage for improvement has pulled down stalls and carved work; and covered, with a thick coat of plaster, column and capital of the most delicate and elaborate workmanship'.[12] Almost no subject escaped the strictures of some guide book or other. Indeed, the 'gentleman of Oxford' who wrote *The New Oxford Guide or Companion Through the University* (1759) laid it down that one function of a guide was 'to direct and assist the judgement of the inquisitive observer', and local antiquaries exercised this function to the full.

The historians who took this task upon themselves were a very mixed bunch. Some held official positions and published greater works of reference, while others made little success of their writings and less of their lives. John Hewitt (1807–78), who held a post in the War Office and enjoyed the society of Bulwer Lytton, Leigh Hunt, Mary Howitt, Mrs S. C. Hall and others, was the author of the *Official Catalogue of the Tower Armories* (1859), a number of standard

72. *A Brief Description of Places of Public Interest, in the County of York:*
country churchyard

works on armour and a popular guide to the Tower of London, published by authority of the Master-General and Board of Ordnance in 1841. His French guide to the Tower reached its thirteenth edition in 1871. On retiring to his native Lichfield he compiled handbooks of local antiquities besides publishing papers in archaeological journals. Edward Jesse (1780–1868), whose main interest was natural history, held a number of official posts, including that of Deputy Surveyor of the Royal Parks and Palaces, which brought him into contact with the restoration work at Hampton Court Palace. He wrote papers on botanical and zoological subjects, and about the royal palaces, including his popular *A Summer's Day at Hampton Court* (1839), which reached a fifth edition by 1842. It was published by John Murray and contained woodcuts by Orlando Jewitt.

Some writers with a very varied career are hard to categorise. Such was Orlando Jewitt's brother, Llewellynn Frederick William Jewitt (1816–86), who is now probably remembered for his *The Ceramic Art of Great Britain, being a history of the ancient and modern porcelain works of the kingdom from prehistoric times* (1877). His earliest training was that of a wood engraver, and he contributed work to the *Illustrated London News* and other periodicals. For a time he worked with his brother, and later was on the staff of *Punch*. From 1849 to 1853 he was chief librarian of Plymouth Public Library, but left and went to Derby to start a monthly penny paper, and in 1860 established the antiquarian journal called the *Reliquary*. His interests in local archaeology and his writings secured his election to the Society of Antiquaries in 1853. His books include *A Guide to the Borough of Derby: with descriptive trips by railway to the most interesting places in the neighbourhood* (1852), for which he draw and engraved the illustrations; *Black's Guide to Derbyshire* (1857); *The Matlock Companion and Visitor's Guide* (c1860); *Black's Guide to Buxton* (1868); *Guide to Alton Towers* (1869); and, with S. C. Hall, *Haddon Hall* (1871).

On a socially higher level was Sir Henry Charles Englefield, FRS, FSA (1752–1822), who wrote guides to Southampton and the Isle of Wight. He was for many years secretary of the Dilettanti Society and a vice-president of the Society of Antiquaries. His other publications were papers on Roman antiquities and astronomy. Another wealthy antiquary but with rather narrower interests was Henry Penruddocke Wyndham, FRS, FSA (1736–1819), who also wrote a guide to the Isle of Wight. He held a number of local offices and interested himself chiefly but not only in the antiquities of his own county of Wiltshire.

Much lower down the social scale were John Price (1773–1801) and John Cole (1792–1848), who tried to earn a living by teaching and bookselling or, as in Cole's case, by bookselling and then by teaching. Price began as a teacher of languages, became a bookseller in Hereford and finally settled at Worcester; his topographical enquiries were stimulated by his local surroundings but not to any great depth of original scholarship. His publications include *The Ludlow Guide* (1797) and a *Worcester Guide* (1799). Cole is credited with the authorship of some hundred publications with whose

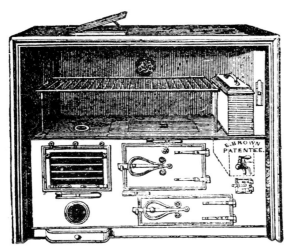

E. BROWN'S IMPROVED PATENT ECONOMICAL
COOKING RANGE,

AND

SELF - ACTING ROASTING APPARATUS,

MANUFACTURED BY

MAPPLEBECK AND LOWE,

BULL RING AND SMITHFIELD, BIRMINGHAM.

This unrivalled invention has been in use several years, and proves that for *economy, simplicity, cleanliness, certain prevention or cure of smoke, safety, elegant appearance,* singular facility of setting and management, capability to make a closed or open fire, together with great solidity of construction, and the superior manner in which it will effect all the necessary culinary operations of the kitchen, *it cannot be equalled.*

This Range has another *highly important advantage,* being set *as a whole,* it does not become a fixture, and can therefore be removed from one house to another. To render the setting, if possible, more simple than it is, the most *clear* and specific printed directions are sent to the country with each Range, so that a mason of the meanest capacity *cannot* commit any error.

The extraordinary sale of this Range has exceeded 1200 in the short space of five years, and is universally allowed to be superior to every other kind in use.

Purchasers are respectfully requested to bear in mind, that they should not calculate the size, and consequently the expense of the Range, by the size of their fireplace, as a smaller Range on this plan will do infinitely more work than a larger one on any other.

☞ Numerous references and testimonials, given in town, and most parts of England, Ireland, Scotland, the West Indies, &c.

printing he seems to have taken special interest and care. He tried to establish himself in Northampton and then in Scarborough. When both these business ventures failed, he took to keeping a school, but all his attempts met with no success. H. R. Tedder notes: 'A self-trained and industrious antiquary, he appears to have been utterly unsuited for the cares of a business life'.

Among those whose livelihoods were affected by railway developments was George Shillibeer (1797–1866), who, in July 1829, first introduced the omnibus into London. Later, in 1834, he ran a service from London to Greenwich and Woolwich, but was ruined by competition from the Greenwich railway. In his later years he became an undertaker and invented a patent hearse (see illustration 48) which considerably reduced the price of funerals. In 1837 he wrote *The "Conducteur", or Visitors' New Guide, to and at Boulogne,* which was published in London by G. S. Tregear of Cheapside

74.   *A Guide to Ripon, Harrogate, etc:* Fountains Abbey

and in Boulogne by Bousfield's newly established Marine Library, which offered English, German, French and other publications at about one-third of the prices in England. Shillibeer introduces himself to his readers as the 'Father of the Metropolitan Omnibus'.

Another tradesman antiquary was John Richard Walbran (1817–69), a wine merchant and mayor of Ripon. His study of Fountains Abbey led to excavations there under his personal direction. His publications include *A Summer's Day at Bolton Priory* (1847) and a very successful guide to Ripon (1844) which reached a ninth (but posthumous) edition in 1871.

Clergy

The Panorama of Plymouth; or, tourist's guide to the principal objects of interest, in the towns and vicinity of Plymouth, Dock, and Stonehouse, written, printed, and published by Samuel Rowe (1793–1853) in 1821 is a good example of a thorough local guide covering most topics succinctly and authoritatively. Rowe's local pride is proclaimed in the quotation on the title page:

> Speak not of Italy—she cannot shew
> A brighter scene than this.

Rowe was apprenticed to a bookseller and his father bought a business for him. He devoted his leisure to literary pursuits and in 1821 became secretary of the Plymouth Institution, then an important centre for artistic and scientific life in Devon; but in the following year he decided to be ordained. Later he held livings in his home county and continued his topographical interests. Perhaps more typical of the host of minor clerical writers is the Rev John Docwra Parry, who died about 1833. He produced a history of Woburn Abbey of which part was reprinted as *A Guide to Woburn Abbey* (1831). In a short life he held minor curacies and published a number of long-forgotten works. The Rev John Pike Jones (1790–1857), with his taste for controversy, serves as another example of a clerical author. He published a *Guide to Scenery in the Neighbourhood of Ashburton* and works on the botany of his county of Devon, as well as other antiquarian and controversial pamphlets.

An incumbent born in the locality he served was in an ideal position to record the customs of his area, and that was important in times of change. In 1837 the Rev William Thornber published his *An Historical and Descriptive Account of Blackpool and Its Neighbourhood*, which includes a glossary of old words used in the Fylde along the coast. Thornber took his duties as parish priest very earnestly, exclaiming 'Oh what tales of spiritual ignorance might I relate'. He goes on to record an evening prayer commonly used by children in the area:

> Matthew, Mark, Luke, and John,
> Bless the bed that I lie on;
> There are four corners to my bed,
> And four angels overspread,
> Two at the feet and two at the head.
> If any ill thing me betide,
> Beneath your wings my body hide.
> Matthew, Mark, Luke, and John,
> Bless the bed that I lie on. Amen

With equal displeasure he also records an ancient custom:

The last evening in October was called the 'Teanlay night', or the fast of All Souls. At the close of that day, till within late years, the hills, which encircle the Fylde, shone brightly with many a bonfire; the mosses of Marton, etc., etc., rivaling them with their fires, kindled for the avowed object of succouring their friends detained in the fancied regions of a middle state. A field, near Poulton, in which the mummery of the 'Teanlays' was once celebrated, (a circle of men standing with bundles of straw, raised on high with forks), is named Purgatory, by the old inhabitants.

Thornber set out to describe what he called the 'mighty changes' which Blackpool had undergone since the writing in 1788 of the earliest guide by William Hutton of Birmingham. The real development of modern Blackpool took place in the second half of the nineteenth century. The railway had reached the town in 1846 but Central Station was not built until 1863; the first pier was erected in the same year. 'Then', says Sir Nikolaus Pevsner, 'things began to happen.' Signs of this are the building in 1867–8 of the Imperial Hydropathic Establishment and other hotels. Thornber would have been astonished at these even mightier changes.

The example of Father West indicates that clergy other than those of the established church contributed to this field of English historical writing. Edmund Butcher (1757–1822) was a unitarian minister whose health forced him to retire to Sidmouth, where he survived for many years producing sermons and a guide. His *A Picture of Sidmouth* reached a fourth edition by 1830 with the title of *A New Guide, Descriptive of the Beauties of Sidmouth.*

75. *The Stranger's Companion in Chester:* the Bridge Gate

PROSPECT HOUSE ACADEMY,
PROSPECT PLACE, HYTHE.
CONDUCTED BY
MR. HENRY HARLEY.

The course of Instruction pursued in this Establishment, embraces the French and Latin Languages, English Grammar, Arithmetic, Merchant's Accounts, Plain and Ornamental Penmanship, Mensuration, Mental Arithmetic, Elocution, Composition, History, Geography, Geometry, Algebra, the Use of the Globes, and the Mathematics. Lectures on various useful and scientific subjects are also delivered regularly to the Pupils.

Every attention is paid to the health, comfort, morals, and general deportment of the Pupils, and the greatest solicitude is manifested to combine scholastic advantages with the comfort of home.

The above Academy is delightfully situated, commanding an extensive view of the sea and the surrounding landscape.

The grounds appropriated for the healthful exercise of the Pupils in playhours are Two Acres in extent.

Sea Bathing in the Season.

Highly respectable London and Country References given.

TERMS.—Boarders under Twelve Years of Age, £20 per Annum; Washing Two Guineas per Annum.

The accomplishments on the Master's Terms. Prospectuses forwarded on application as above.

A Quarter's Notice previous to the removal of a Pupil, and the usual etceteras required.

MRS. HARLEY'S
SEMINARY FOR YOUNG LADIES,
PROSPECT PLACE, HYTHE.

The course of Instruction adopted in this Establishment embraces the usual course of an English Education, together with French (by a Parisian), Drawing and the accomplishments. Mrs. H. begs to observe, that the Pupils entrusted to her care are treated as members of one family; their health is anxiously watched over: while her system of imparting instruction, (suggested by experience), ensures their daily advancement in the respective branches of study or usefulness, in which, according to circumstances, they may be engaged. Habits of neatness and order are promoted, and the conscientious discharge of duty rendered inseparable from their happiness.

The Young Ladies are conducted in fine weather for walking exercises in the beautiful district by which Hythe is bordered, or upon the sea-shore. Sea-bathing from the Machines.

TERMS.—Boarders £20 per Annum, Washing £2.

The Young Ladies are instructed in writing and arithmetic by Mr. Harley, and the accomplishments by Masters.

Prospectuses forwarded upon application, and satisfactory references given if required.

In this formative period of the English guide book, there were those who attempted more than one guide and publishers who tried a series, but the genre was as yet uncodified and, although there was a generally agreed range and depth of topics to be covered, room remained for individual taste and enterprise to flourish.

Bibliographical Notes and References

Introduction

1. The fact that the royal library at Balmoral in the 1860s contained '26 guide books, 32 *Ladies of the Lake* and 12 *Rob Roys*' (E. Longford. *Victoria R. I.* [1966], 467) rather supports this view.

1 Travellers and Travelling

1. See G. F. Barwick. 'Some Early Guide Books', *Trans of the Bibliographical Soc*, vol 7 (1904), 191–207
2. *The New History, Survey and Description of the City and Suburbs of Bristol* (1794), 101
3. First published in 1766 with many subsequent editions. Reprinted by Adams & Dart (1970), with introduction by K. G. Ponting
4. A. B. Granville. *The Spas of England and Principal Sea-bathing Places* (1841); J. A. R. Pimlott. *The Englishman's Holiday: a social history* (1947); K. Lindley. *Coastline* (1967), 35–43; R. L. P. and D. M. Jowitt. *Discovering Spas* (1971)
5. 4th ed (1808), preface
6. Quoted in R. Pearsall. *The Worm in the Bud* (1971), 65
7. T. K. Glazebrook. *A Guide to Southport*, 2nd ed (1826), 61
8. See Pimlott, 211–37
9. W. T. Moncrieff. *The Visitor's New Guide to the Spa of Leamington Priors* (1818), 8
10. *The Picture of London for 1804*, 378. An anti-Semitic element is common in these warnings. William Kidd's *London and Its Dangers* [c1835], 36, claims of the 'Lady Abbesses', ie keepers of brothels, that 'most of them are Jewesses'

11. *Cruchley's Picture of London*, 3rd ed (1838), 175–6

12. T. E. Jones. *A Descriptive Account of the Literary Works of John Britton, F.S.A., etc., etc., etc.* (1849), 77

13. J. J. Tobias. *Crime and Industrial Society in the Nineteenth Century*, 2nd ed (1972), 140

14. *The Girlhood of Queen Victoria: a selection from Her Majesty's diaries between the years 1832 and 1840*, vol 1 (1912), 43

15. T. Dick. *On the Improvement of Society by Diffusion of Knowledge*, 2nd ed (1834), 530–31

16. W. Ames. *Prince Albert and Victorian Taste* (1967), 48

17. *Parry's Railway Companion from Chester to Holyhead*, 2nd ed (1849), 13 (facsimile reprint, 1970)

18. See C. M. L. Bouch and G. P. Jones. *A Short Economic and Social History of the Lake Counties 1500–1830.* (1961), 282

19. See M. Robbins. *The Railway Age* (1962)

20. See J. P. Anderson. *The Book of British Topography* (1881), 34–6, and G. Ottley. *A Bibliography of British Railway History* (1965), section T

21. W. Wordsworth. *A Guide Through the District of the Lakes*, 5th ed (1835), 67. See also M. Moorman. *William Wordsworth: a Biography—the Later Years* (1965)

2 Abroad

1. See R. S. Lambert (ed). *Grand Tour: a journey in the tracks of the age of aristocracy* (1935)

2. C. H. Timperley. *A Dictionary of Printers and Printing* (1839), 918

3. J. J. Barnes 'Galignani and the publication of English books in France: a postscript' in *The Library*, 5th series, vol. 25 (1970) 294–312

4. *Paris in All Its Glory; a new pocket companion in a visit to Paris*, nd [c1835], 23

5. S. Smiles. *A Publisher and His Friends: memoir and correspondence of the late John Murray*, vol 2 (1891), 460

6. Smiles, 151–2

7. Reprinted by University of Leicester Press (1970), with introduction by Prof J. Simmons

8. Reprinted by David & Charles (1971)

9. See E. W. Gilbert. 'Richard Ford and His "Hand-book for Travellers in Spain",' *Geographical Journal*, vol 106 (1945), 144–51

10. P. F. Anson. *The Call of the Cloister* (1964), 337

11. W. Walsh. *The History of the Romeward Movement in the Church of England 1833–1864* (1900), 364–5

12. Some further examples of the development of Murray's guide books in England, in Europe and beyond (although the most exotic come outside the period being considered here), are 1836, *A Handbook for Travellers on the Continent*; 1837, Southern Germany; 1838, Switzerland; 1839, Denmark; 1840, Greece; 1842, Northern Italy; 1843, France, Central Italy; 1845, Spain; 1847, Egypt; 1851, Devon, London; 1853, Southern Italy; 1855, Portugal; 1856, Wiltshire; 1858, Rome, Surrey, Syria; 1859, India; 1860, Berkshire, South Wales; 1861, North Wales; 1864, Durham, Ireland, Paris, Sicily; 1865, Russia; 1866, English Lakes; 1867, Gloucestershire, Scotland, Tyrol, Yorkshire; 1868, Derbyshire; 1870, Essex, Shropshire; 1871, Constantinople; 1873, Algeria; 1875, Sweden; 1877, Sussex; and 1878, Northamptonshire. During the 1860s Murray published a number of *Knapsack Guides*. These were shorter and cheaper versions of the *Handbooks*. This was not a new idea, but there seems to have been a demand for them, although not to the extent of surpassing the main works.

13. The progress of Black's series of guides can be illustrated by the dates of first publication of some examples: 1839, Edinburgh, Glasgow; 1841, the English Lakes; 1843, England and Wales; 1850, London to Edinburgh; 1851, Wales; 1853, Trossachs; 1854, Aberdeen, Belfast, Dublin, Ireland, Killarney; 1855, Derbyshire, Devonshire, Hampshire; 1857, North Wales, Warwickshire; 1858, Yorkshire; 1860, Gloucestershire, Kent; 1861, Surrey; 1865, Channel Isles; 1866, Brighton, Guernsey, Jersey; 1867, Norway, Paris; 1868, Buxton, Leamington, Leeds, Manchester, Scarborough; 1869, Italy; 1876, Cornwall, Nottinghamshire; and 1877, Rhine, Switzerland

14. E. Liveing. *Adventure in Publishing: the House of Ward, Lock, 1854–1954* (1954), 69

15. Reprinted for the London Topographical Society by the University Press, Cambridge, in 1951

16. Timperley, 760

17. 8th ed (1834), 197

3 At Home

1. See E. Moir. *The Discovery of England: the English tourist 1540 to 1840* (1964), which has a very useful bibliography, especially for the earlier part of the period
2. See Gwynfryn Walters. *The Tourist and Guide Book Literature of Wales 1770–1870: a descriptive and bibliographic survey with an analysis of the cartographic content and its context*, University of Wales MSc thesis (1966)
3. W. T. Moncrieff. *The Visitors' New Guide to the Spa of Leamington Priors*, 3rd ed (1824), 220
4. Moncrieff, 218
5. R. B. Wilson. 'The Evolution of Local History Writing on Warwickshire', *Birmingham Archaeological Soc Trans and Proc for the Year 1953*, vol 71 (1955), 74
6. Leigh. *Guide to the Lakes and Mountains of Cumberland, Westmorland, and Lancashire*, 3rd ed (1835), vii–viii
7. See Moir, 139
8. N. Nicholson. *The Lakers: the adventures of the tourists* (1955), 63
9. Walters, vol 1, 8
10. T. West. *A Guide to the Lakes in Cumberland, Westmorland, and Lancashire*, 2nd ed (1780), 12. My italics
11. J. Drake. *Picture of Birmingham* (1825), 16. 'Some of our most interesting manufactures have been hermetically sealed against all visitants'
12. *Cruchley's Picture of London*, 174

4 The Guides

1. Smiles, 463
2. In 1859 Nelson's produced their *Hand-books for Tourists*. This undistinguished series included volumes on Abbotsford, Western Highlands, English Lakes, Edinburgh, Lakes of Killarney, Oban, Staffa, and Iona, *The River Thames from Oxford to the Sea*, Windsor and Eton, Kew, etc, Isle of Wight, and Stratford-on-Avon. They contained 'oil-colour pictures' of a blue and purplish character. Nelson's sold such pictures by the packet at 1s or 1s 6d, bound in cloth. (The custom survives in Europe, rather than in England, of selling packets of picture postcards

with a slight letterpress introduction. The most delightful ones come from the USSR.)

A decade later there *Nelson's Pictorial Guide books for Tourists*. This was a slim series with travellers' information, but the illustrations were the main selling point. The cover title was *Nelson's View-books for Tourists*. Some examples are, for 1869 Carnarvon and Snowdon, Isle of Man, Isle of Wight (four parts), London—the West End, Mont Blanc (no text), *Sights near London, A Trip on the Thames from Blackfriars to the Nore;* for 1870 Folkestone, Portsmouth; for 1871 *International Exhibition*, Salt Lake City; and for 1872, with the title *Nelson's Oil Colour Views*, books like *The Yosemite Valley, and the Mammoth Trees and Geysers of California.* These were even less distinguised than the earlier series.

3. Some examples of their publications are *Cook's Scottish Tourist Official Directory. A guide to the system of tours in Scotland, under the direction of the principal railway, steamboat, and coach companies* (1861), and *Guide to Cook's Excursions to Paris; and directory of excursions and tours in Switzerland and Italy* (1865). After Cook took his son into partnership, the firm published such handbooks as, in 1874, Florence, Holland, Switzerland; 1875, Italy; 1876, Black Forest, Egypt, Palestine; 1877, London; and 1878, Paris, Riviera

4. P. H. Fitzgerald. *The Story of 'Bradshaw's Guide'* (1890), 15–16

5. The publisher of John Wilkes's notorious *North Briton*

6. W. J. Rees. *The Hereford Guide*, 3rd ed (1827), preface to the first edition

7. H. W. Hamilton. *Doctor Syntax: a silhouette of William Combe, Esq (1742–1823)* (1969), 243–61

8. See H. W. Hodgson. *A Bibliography of the History and Topography of Cumberland and Westmorland* (1968)

9. See J. J. Bagley. *Historical Interpretation. 2 Sources of English History 1540 to the present day* (1971), 191–7; and M. J. Moore-Rinvolucri, 'Background Material in a Guide Book', *Canadian Modern Languages Review* (May 1972), 26–8

10. See J. E. Norton. *Guide to the National and Provincial Directories of England and Wales, Excluding London, Published Before 1856* (1950), 61

11. Norton, 92–4

12. P. Morgan. *Warwickshire Printers' Notices 1799–1866* (1970), 38

13. J. Simmons. *Parish and Empire: Studies and Sketches* (1952), 106

14. P. B. Chatwin. 'Early Guide Books to St Mary's Church,

Warwick', *Trans of the Birmingham Archaeological Soc*, vol 65 (1949) 41–4

15. T. Rees. *Reminiscences of Literary London from 1779 to 1853 . . . with extensive additions by John Britton* (1896), 157

16. E. S. de Beer. 'The Development of the Guide-book until the Early Nineteenth Century', *Journal of the British Archaeological Assoc*, 3rd series, vol 15 (1952), 36

17. Joshua 18:9

5 *Readers and Guide Books*

1. The royal menagerie was established in the Tower by Henry III and remained there until 1834

2. *The Gloucester New Guide* (1802), 56

3. D. Read. *Press and People 1790–1850* (1961), 20

4. J. Ainsworth. *A Guide to Scarborough*, 7th ed (1832), 43

5. See J. H. Treble. 'Liverpool Working-class Housing, 1801–1851', S. D. Chapman (ed). *The History of Working Class Housing: a Symposium* (1971), 168

6. Read, 12

7. In T. H. Shepherd. *Bath and Bristol, with the Counties of Somerset and Gloucester, Displayed in a Series of Views* (1829, reprinted by F. Graham, 1969)

8. B. J. Ronchetti. *Antiquarian and Archaeological Scholarship in Warwickshire 1800–1860*, University of Birmingham MA thesis (1952), 18

9. Reprinted 1969 by Kingsmead Bookshop, Bath

10. Abel Heywood's series of penny guides began in 1866, and the following selection of places will show the progress made: 1866, Buxton, Belle Vue Zoological Gardens, Manchester, Scarborough, Southport; 1867, Brighton, Chatsworth, Isle of Wight, Kenilworth, Liverpool, Manchester; 1868, Bath, Hampton Court, Malvern, Oxford, Portsmouth, and *A Guide to Leeds Exhibition of Ancient and Modern Pictures, Works of Arts, etc.*; 1869, Alton Towers, Hastings, Weston-super-Mare, Worksop and Sherwood Forest; 1870, *Half-holiday Trips Around Manchester, Inland Spas of England, Southern Watering-places*, Reading, Sheffield, Whalley Abbey; 1871, Hull; 1872, Kent, *Watering-places of North-eastern Coast. Abel Heywood's Tourists Guides* were based on this series

11. G. Pollard. 'Changes in the Style of Bookbinding, 1550–1830', *The Library*, 5th series, vol 11 (1956), 78 and 83

6 The Producers

1. E. H. Cordeaux and D. H. Merry. *A Bibliography of Printed Works Relating to the University of Oxford* (1968)

2. Bath Municipal Libraries. *Bath Guides, Directories and Newspapers in the Reference Library*, rev ed (1967)

3. Smiles, 445

4. A. T. Patterson. *A History of Southampton 1700–1914, vol 1: an Oligarchy in Decline 1700–1835* (1966), 41–2 and 114–15

5. 24th ed (1826), edited by John Britton, and again in 1827, 1830, and 1833

6. *The Critic* (24 March 1860), 368

7. Jones, 142, and *Gentleman's Magazine*, vol 87, pt 2 (1817), 537

8. Jones, 76–9

9. Timperley, 951

10. Timperley, 774

11. D. Blakey. *The Minerva Press 1790–1820* (1939)

12. M. Plant. *The English Book Trade: an economic history of the making and sale of books*, 2nd ed (1965), 404

13. Pigot & Co. *National Commercial Directory*, vol 3 (1830), 749

14. W. B. Todd. *A Directory of Printers and Others in Allied Trades: London and Vicinity 1800–1840* (1972), xxiii–xxiv

15. Morgan, xxiii

16. Ronchetti, 190

17. Timperley, 883

18. Timperley, 869

19. J. A. Picton. *Memorials of Liverpool, Historical and Topographical*, vol 2 (1907), 16

20. T. Kelly. *Early Public Libraries: a history of public libraries in Great Britain before 1850* (1966)

21. P. Kaufman. 'The English Community Library: a chapter in English social history', *Trans of the American Philosophical Soc*, ns, vol 57, pt 7 (1967), 11–13

22. J. E. Vaughan. 'Contrasts in Ideas for Library Provision in Early Nineteenth Century England', *The Library Assoc Record*, vol 68 (1966), 45–9

23. P. Matthias. *English Trade Tokens* (1962), plate 15(5)

24. Interior illustrated by Kaufman, Fig 7

25. *Scenery of Great Britain and Ireland in Aquatint and Lithography 1770–1860 from the Library of J. R. Abbey: a bibliographical catalogue*, vol 1 (1952), 76

26. Plant, 315–16

27. M. Twyman. *Lithography 1800–1850: the techniques of drawing on stone in England and France and their application in works of topography* (1970), 178

28. Twyman, 183

29. Morgan, 32–3

30. J. M. G. Blakiston. 'Winchester College Library in the Eighteenth and Nineteenth Centuries', *The Library*, 5th series, vol 17 (1962), 23–45

31. G. L. Keynes. *William Pickering: Publisher. A memoir and a hand-list of his editions* (1924), 58; and Blakiston

32. H. Carter. *Orlando Jewitt* (1962), 2

33. Carter, 40

34. H. Cole. *Fifty Years of Public Work*, vol 1 (1884), 102

35. Vol 2 (1838), plate 79

36. P. Muir. *Victorian Illustrated Books* (1971), 20

7 The Authors

1. M. Moorman. *William Wordsworth: a Biography—the Later Years* (1965), 161 and 595–6. The 1835 text was reprinted in 1951 with illustrations by John Piper and an introduction by the Rev Professor W. M. Merchant.

2. Cordeaux and Merry, no 298

3. E. Quayle. *Ballantyne the Brave: a Victorian Writer and His Family* (1967), 123

4. See S. Halket & J. Laing. *A Dictionary of the Anonymous and Pseudononymous Literature of Great Britain*, 4 vols (1882–8)

5. Read, 78–9

6. E. Longford, *Victoria R.I.* (1966), 103

7. R. K. Webb. *Harriet Martineau: a Radical Victorian* (1960)

8. S. Watts. *A Walk Through Leicester; being a guide to strangers* (1804), 37 (reprinted by Leicester University Press, 1967)

9. E. Lee. *The Watering Places of England*, 4th ed (1859), preface

10. A. Hunter. *The Waters of Harrogate and Its Vicinity*, 4th ed (1834), 88

11.   A. Smith. *The Harrogate Medical Guide; a popular and practical treatise on the mineral waters of Harrogate, and the diseases in which they are useful; with supplementary remarks on diet and exercise; and some select cases*, 2nd ed (1847), 18 and 19

12.   7th ed (1844), 191–2

ources of Illustrations

1. *A Hand-book for Visitors to Oxford* (1847). From the title page. Woodcut by Orlando Jewitt. 67 × 83 mm.
2. Official advertiser, p 9 in G. Measom. *The Official Illustrated Guide to the Bristol and Exeter, North and South Devon, Cornwall, and South Wales Railways* (c1860). Interior of Cyclops Iron and Steel Works, Sheffield. 100 × 146 mm.
3. *The Hastings Guide*, 5th ed (1821). Title page. 143 × 84 mm.
4. *Black's Guide Book Advertiser 1848–1849*, 22. From advertisement for Croall's Royal Mail and General Coach Establishment. Probably a stock block. 19 × 50 mm.
5. John Feltham. *A Guide to All the Watering and Sea-bathing Places; with a description of the Lakes; a sketch of a tour in Wales; and itineraries* (1803), facing 36. 76 × 117 mm.
6. *The Original Bath Guide: containing an essay on the Bath Waters; with a description of the city, and a variety of useful information* (1841), facing 21. 60 × 78 mm.
7. Feltham, facing 367. 68 × 115 mm.
8. E. Wallis. *Wallis's Brighton Townsman and Visitor's Directory; describing the recent improvements, libraries, natural productions, hotels and inns, places of worship, charitable institutions, and bye laws of the town. To which is prefixed a brief history of the county and advice to bathers* (1826), frontispiece. 98 × 158 mm.
9. W. Kidd. *The Picturesque Pocket Companion to Margate, Ramsgate, Broadstairs, and the Parts Adjacent* (1831), 77. Wood engraving by G. W. Bonner. See 6 and 67. 41 × 61 mm.
10. *The Milton and Gravesend Guide: detailing the principal objects of interest in the excursion from London to that popular watering-place; a description of Gravesend, Milton, and their environs; and an account of the return by land to the metropolis*, 2nd ed [c1830], frontispiece. 100 × 126 mm.

11. R. Starratt. *The Stranger's Guide Through Dublin, containing practical directions for the easy perambulation of the city, and for the inspection of public buildings, institutions, and establishments*, new ed (1849), 116. 78 × 88 mm.

12. *The New Illustrated Hand-book to Folkestone, and its picturesque neighbourhood, with a description of the South Eastern Railway* (1848), [185–6]. 140 × 73 mm.

13. *The Original Bath Guide: containing an essay on the Bath waters, with a description of the city, and a variety of useful information* (1844), facing 60. 80 × 118 mm.

14. J. Furby. *Furby's Hand-book for Strangers Visiting Bridlington-Quay, and a descriptive guide to the most interesting scenery in the neighbourhood* (1846), 51. 11 × 56 mm.

15. *The Picturesque Hand-book to Liverpool; a manual for the resident and visitor, being a new and greatly improved edition of the Stranger's pocket guide*, fourth thousand (1842), 73. 44 × 65 mm.

16. *The Picturesque Hand-book to Liverpool*, etc. [143]. 46 × 47 mm.

17. D. Hughson. *Walks Through London Including Westminster and the Borough of Southwark, with the surrounding suburbs . . . forming a complete guide to the British metropolis* (1817), facing 107. 105 × 67 mm.

18. *Parry's Railway Companion from Chester to Holyhead; containing a descriptive and historical account of all objects of interest that present themselves on this beautifully picturesque line: especially the monster tubular bridges across the River Conway and the Menai Straits, and the Herculean harbour of refuge at Holyhead. To which is added, the tourist's guide to Dublin and its environs*, 2nd ed (1849), 132–3. 130 × 165 mm.

19. *The New Illustrated Hand-book to Folkestone*, etc, between 116 and 117. 118 × 148 mm.

20. *The Picturesque Hand-book to Liverpool*, etc, facing 72. Entrance screen of Lime Street Station, now demolished, designed by J. Foster, junior, in 1836. Liverpool Corporation contributed £2,000 to the beautifying of this façade. 90 × 141 mm.

21. *Chilcott's Descriptive History of Bristol, Ancient and Modern; or, a guide to Bristol, Clifton, and the Hotwells: with topographical notices of the neighbouring villages*, etc, 7th ed (1846), 10. 43 × 72 mm. Now a

minor part of Temple Meads Station; built in 1839–40 and an example of the GWR's architectural taste which so incensed Pugin.

22. S. W. Theakston. *Theakston's Guide to Scarborough: comprising a brief sketch of the antiquities, natural productions, and romantic scenery, of the town and neighbourhood*, 5th ed (1854), 112. 12 × 56 mm.

23. Wallis, 68. 44 × 62 mm.

24. W. C. F. G. Sheridan. *A Topographical and Historical Guide to the Isle of Wight, containing every information interesting to the antiquarian, botanist, geologist, and tourist; with biographical notice of eminent natives; remarks on the climate; the sandrock chalybeate spring; the rate of passage, etc*, 2nd ed (1833), facing 129. 102 × 138 mm.

25. *Galignani's New Paris Guide . . . arranged on an entirely new plan* (1848), [i]. 71 × 122 mm.

26. E. Jesse. *A Summer's Day at Hampton Court, being a guide to the palace and gardens; with an illustrated catalogue of the pictures*, 4th ed (1841), [152]. 144 × 78 mm.

27. *Handbook for Westmorland, Cumberland, and the Lakes*, 2nd ed (1869), 25. 153 × 89 mm.

28. T. Michell. *Handbook for Travellers in Russia, Poland, and Finland*, new ed (1865), 152–3. 128 × 95 mm.

29. *The Picturesque Hand-book to Liverpool*, etc, 10. 25 × 52 mm.

30. *The Windsor Guide, with a Brief Account of Eton*, new ed (1825), frontispiece. 95 × 127 mm.

31. S. Leigh. *Leigh's New Picture of London: or, a view of the political, religious, medical, literary, municipal, commercial and moral state, of the British metropolis: presenting a brief and luminous guide to the stranger, on all subjects connected with general information, business or amusement*, 2nd ed (1818), facing 497. 55 × 102 mm.

32. *Chilcott's Descriptive History of Bristol*, etc, frontispiece. 86 × 120 mm.

33. *The Oxford University and City Guide, on a New Plan: containing a full description of the colleges, halls, public buildings, libraries, gardens, walks, pictures and statues in Oxford; with an account of the dresses, examinations, degrees . . . to which is added a guide to Blenheim and Nuneham*, new ed (1831), facing 108. 89 × 135 mm.

34. J. Otley. *A Descriptive Guide to the English Lakes, and Adjacent Mountains: with notices of the botany, mineralogy, and geology of the district*, 8th ed (1850), facing 6. [Originally] '. . . sketches, by the

Author's own unpractised hand, of the most remarkable Ranges of Mountains surrounding the different Lakes, as they appear from select stations on the roads, or places of easy access . . . [In later editions] . . . intrusted to experienced artists; and has latterly been considered so necessary an adjunct to a work of this kind, that it has been unreservedly imitated in rival publications' [p iv of preface]. 78 × 150 mm.

35. Kidd. *The Picturesque Pocket Companion*, etc, facing 66. Margate gasometer 'is a neat and elegant building, situate in the Dane, built after a Grecian model, and erected in 1824, at which period Margate was first lighted with gas'. 57 × 95 mm.

36. Sheridan, title page. 141 × 83 mm.

37. S. Glover. *The Peak Guide, containing the topographical, statistical, and general history of Buxton, Chatsworth, Edensor, Castlteon [sic], Bakewell, Haddon, Matlock, and Cromford*, ed T. Noble (1830), XL. 126 × 109 mm.

38. *Black's Guide to England and Wales containing plans of the principal cities, charts, maps and views, and a list of hotels* (1870), 502–3. 145 × 205 mm.

39. W. Kidd. *Kidd's New Guide to the 'Lions' of London; or, the strangers directory, etc, etc* (1832), 11. Engraved by G. W. Bonner. 33 × 58 mm.

40. S. Leigh. *Leigh's New Picture of England and Wales, comprehending a description of the principal towns, ancient remains, natural and artificial curiosities, soil and produce, agriculture, manufactures, rivers, and canals, principal seats, bathing places, etc.* [Edited by T. G. B.] (1820), facing 576.

41. *The Route Book of Devon: a guide for the stranger and tourist, to the towns, watering places, and other interesting localities of this county*, 2nd ed (1846), 170–71. 122 × 160 mm.

42. W. J. Rees. *The Hereford Guide: containing a concise history of the city of Hereford . . . and a particular account of the schools, mails, stage coaches, waggons and roads*, 3rd ed (1827), facing 61. 78 × 113 mm.

43. *The Stranger in Liverpool; or, an historical and descriptive view of the town of Liverpool and its environs*, 12th ed (1839), facing 15. 79 × 127 mm.

44. *Murray's Handbook for Devon and Cornwall (1859)* (1971), 217. 148 × 89 mm.

45. *The Manchester Guide. A brief historical description of the towns of Manchester and Salford, the public buildings, and the charitable and literary institutions* (1804), frontispiece. 205 × 256 mm.

46. W. Cornish. *Cornish's Stranger's Guide Through Birmingham. Being an accurate description of all that is worthy the notice of the visitor to the town, either in its public buildings, manufactories, or religious edifices, with the public walks and rides in the vicinity, etc* (1844), facing 44. 118 × 134 mm.

47. J. Feltham. *The Picture of London, for 1810; being a correct guide to all the curiosities, amusements, exhibitions, public establishments, and remarkable objects, in and near London,* 11th ed (1810), facing 352 [sic]. 118 × 228 mm.

48. T. Cook. *A Guide to Leicester . . . with an almanack for 1843, with county information, etc* (1843), [133]. Section entitled 'Cook's Leicester Permanent Advertiser', see 77. 155 × 89 mm.

49. A. Freeling. *The Windsor Railway Companion; and guide to the castle and town; to Eton and its college and to Virginia Water* (1840), [74]. 117 × 69 mm.

50. Freeling. *The Windsor Railway Companion, etc,* [69]. 128 × 74 mm.

51. *The New Bristol Guide* (1804), [190]. Guide printed for and sold by W. Sheppard. Printed by R. Edwards. 142 × 78 mm.

52. Cornish, facing 40. 134 × 91 mm.

53. *A Historical Description of Westminster Abbey; its monuments and curiosities* (1843), title page. 153 × 76 mm.

54. *The New Illustrated Hand-book to Folkestone, etc,* [202]. 140 × 73 mm.

55. W. Batcheller. *The New Dover Guide, including a concise sketch of the ancient and modern history of the town and castle, with such other general information as may be useful to visitors; and a short description of the neighbouring villages,* 5th ed (1842), [191]. 130 × 93 mm. Guide printed and published by the author and his King's Arms Library.

56. Batcheller, 149. 50 × 66 mm. 'The King's Arms Library, No. 1. Snargate-street, near the Parade, was erected by W. Batcheller in 1826. The circulating library contains 5143 volumes, embracing every branch of English literature; and new publications are continually adding to the number. A handsome room is fitted up for the accommodation of subscribers; and the table is constantly supplied with six daily, and thirteen weekly and provincial papers, besides magazines,

reviews, etc. Adjoining the library is a stationery shop. . . . The Dover Club have reading and billiard rooms over the shop and library, elegantly fitted up, and also adjoining card and dressing rooms.'

57. *The Hastings Guide*, frontispiece. 100 × 156 mm. J. Barry of the Marine Library published this guide. 'Over the Library is a very good Billiard Room, from which there is a fine view of the sea. Next the Library is the Marine Cottage, a very desirable Lodging House, particularly for invalids during the winter' (p 38).

58. W. T. Moncrieff. *The Visitors' New Guide to the Spa of Leamington Priors, and Its Vicinity . . . with poetical illustrations, and an analysis and professional dissertation upon the nature, properties, and cures performed by the waters*, 3rd ed (1824), facing vii. Guide printed and published at Elliston's British and Foreign Library. 76 × 110 mm.

59. P. Hall. *Ductor Vindogladiensis. An Historical and Descriptive Guide to the Town of Wimborne Minster, Dorsetshire* (1830), verso of title page. See 64. 52 × 45 mm.

60. *The New Bristol Guide*, frontispiece. 75 × 136 mm.

61. J. Otley. *A Descriptive Guide to the English Lakes, and Adjacent Mountains: with notices of the botany, mineralogy, and geology of the district*, 7th ed (1844), 192. Kirkby Lonsdale church, engraved by Orlando Jewitt. See 65 and 74. 37 × 78 mm. 62 × 68 mm.

62. *A Hand-book for Visitors to Oxford*, 207. View of Worcester College, Oxford. 62 × 93 mm.

63. Kidd. *The Picturesque Pocket Companion, etc*, facing 64. Margate Market. 58 × 95 mm.

64. A. Freeling. *Picturesque Excursions; containing upwards of four hundred views at and near places of popular resort; with descriptions of each locality* (1839), 280. 60 × 101 mm.

65. Kidd. *The Picturesque Pocket Companion, etc*, 70. 18 × 48 mm. Also on title page of Kidd. *New Guide to the "Lions"*, etc.

66. J. Phillips. *Black's Picturesque Guide to the English Lakes including the geology of the district*, 15th ed (1868), 53. Home of William Wordsworth. 81 × 128 mm.

67. *The Oxford University and City Guide, on a New Plan: containing a full description of the colleges, halls, public buildings, libraries, gardens, walks, pictures and statues in Oxford; with an account of the dresses, examinations, degrees . . . to which is added a guide to Blenheim . . .*,

new ed (1835), facing 74. 88 × 108 mm. The prize poem 'Palestine' by Reginald Heber (1783–1826), Bishop of Calcutta, was received with great enthusiasm when first recited in the Sheldonian in 1803.

68. J. Beck. *Beck's Leamington Guide; with an historical and descriptive account of the neighbourhood, including . . . prices of cars and phaetons*, 9th ed (1849), [161]. Engraved by W. T. Bonner. 59 × 86 mm.

69. *The Cambridge Guide: with a description and history of the colleges, halls, libraries, museums, and other public buildings, with the ceremonies and customs of the town and university, and a short account of Ely cathedral*, new ed (1840), facing 41. 86 × 145 mm.

70. Theakston, 197. 32 × 51 mm.

71. E. Lee. *The Watering Places of England; with a summary of their medical topography and remedial resources*, 4th ed (1859), 308. 118 × 76 mm.

72. A. E. Hargrove. *A Brief Description of Places of Public Interest, in the County of York within Twenty Six Miles of the City* (1843), 186. 27 × 45 mm.

73. Cornish, 96. 113 × 66 mm.

74. J. R. Walbran. *A Guide to Ripon, Harrogate, Fountains Abbey, Bolton Priory, and several places of interest in their vicinity*, 5th ed (1851), 78. Fountains Abbey. 62 × 53 mm.

75. *The Stranger's Companion in Chester: including a description of Eaton Hall*, 6th ed (1833), 81. 36 × 63 mm.

76. *The New Illustrated Hand-book to Folkestone*, [199]. 140 × 73 mm.

77. G. Measom. *The Official Illustrated Guide to the North-Western Railway (Including the Chester and Holyhead Line), and All Their Branches: including descriptions of the most important manufactories in the large towns on the lines* (c1859), 20. 90 × 110 mm.

78. G. Measom. *The Official Illustrated Guide to the Great Western Railway* (c1860), 872. 33 × 45 mm.

79. Phillips, rear endpapers. 144 × 98 mm.

Endpapers

J. Feltham. *A Guide to All the Watering and Sea-bathing Places*. New Edition (1810), facing 492. 140 × 188 mm.

Initial Letters

p13 J. Hewitt. *The Tower: its history, armories, and antiquities . . . now first compiled from official documents in the Tower*, 2nd ed (1845), ix. Each chapter opens with initial letter in a variety of styles. Drawings of armour by the author. 68 × 55 mm.

p148 W. F. Wakeman. *Archaeologia Hibernica. A hand-book of Irish antiquities, pagan and Christian: especially of such as are easy of access from the Irish metropolis* (1848), 48. Each chapter opens with initial letter in Celtic style. Illustrations by author engraved by George Hanlon of Rathgar. 68 × 20 mm.

77. *The Official Illustrated Guide to the North-Western Railway:* Camden Town engine-house, the 'Roundhouse'

Select Bibliography

Social background

Addison, W. *English Spas* (1951)
Clark, K. *The Gothic Revival: an essay in the history of taste,* rev ed (1962)
Freeling, A. *Picturesque Excursions* (1839)
Hern, A. *The Seaside Holiday: the history of the English seaside resort* (1967)
Jowitt, R. L. P. and D. M. *Discovering Spas* (1971)
Manning-Saunders, R. *Seaside England* (1951)
Moir, E. *The Discovery of England: the English tourist 1540 to 1840* (1964)
Nicholson, N. *The Lakers: the adventures of the tourists* (1955)
Pimlott, J. A. R. *The Englishman's Holiday: a social history* (1947)
Robbins, M. *The Railway Age* (1962)
Stokes, H. G. *The Very First History of the English Seaside* (1947)

Printing and publishing

Adam & Charles Black 1807–1957: some chapters in the history of a publishing house (1957)
Carter, J. *Binding Variants in English Publishing 1820–1900* (1932)
Gray, N. *Nineteenth Century Ornamental Types and Title Pages* (1938)
Lewis, J. *Printed Ephemera* (1962)
McLean, R. *Victorian Book Design,* 2nd ed (1972)
Plant, M. *The English Book Trade: an economic history of the making and sale of books,* 2nd ed (1965)
Ramsden, C. *Bookbinders of the United Kingdom (Outside London) 1780–1840* (1954)
Sadleir, M. *The Evolution of Publishers' Binding Styles 1770–1900* (1930)
Timperley, C. H. *A Dictionary of Printers and Printing* (1839)
Twyman, M. *Lithography 1800–1850: the techniques of drawing on stone in England and France and their application in works of topography* (1970)
Twyman, M. *Printing 1770–1970: an illustrated history of its development and uses in England* (1970)

County and other bibliographies listing guides

The value of many topographical bibliographies is limited. In some, guides are hard to locate except by very thorough searching, and in others, especially some of the older works, guides are considered to be beneath serious attention. Catalogues, published or otherwise, of local history collections in libraries are of particular importance.

Anderson, J. P. *The Book of English Topography* (1881)

Austin, R. *Catalogue of the Gloucestershire Collection* (1928)

Bartholomew, A. T. *Catalogue of the Books and Papers for the Most Part Relating to . . . Cambridge Bequeathed to the University by John Willis Clark, M.A.* (1912)

Bath Municipal Libraries. *Bath Guides, Directories and Newspapers in the Reference Library*, rev ed (1967)

Birmingham City Public Libraries. *A Catalogue of the Birmingham Collection* (1918), and *Supplement 1918–1931* (1931)

Bowes, R. *A Catalogue of Books Printed at or Relating to the University and County of Cambridge from 1521 to 1893 with Bibliographical and Biographical Notes*, 2 vols (1894)

Cordeaux, E. H. and Merry, D. H. *A Bibliography of Printed Works Relating to the University of Oxford* (1968)

Corns, A. R. *Bibliotheca Lincolniensis: a catalogue of the books, pamphlets, etc. relating to the city and county of Lincoln, preserved in the reference department of the City of Lincoln Public Library* (1904)

Davison, J. V. *Bibliotheca Devoniensis: a catalogue of the printed books relating to the county of Devon* (1852), and *Supplement* (1861)

Fishwick, H. *The Lancashire Library: a bibliographical account of books on topography, biography, history and miscellaneous literature relating to the County Palatine, etc* (1875)

Fordham, H. G. *The Road-books and Itineraries of Great Britain, 1570 to 1850: catalogue with an introduction and a bibliography* (1924)

Fussell, G. E. *The Exploration of England: a select bibliography of travel and topography: 1570–1815* (1935)

Goss, C. W. F. *The London Directories 1677–1855: a bibliography with notes on their origin and development* (1932)

Green, E. *Bibliotheca Somersetensis: a catalogue of books, pamphlets, single sheets and broadsheets in some way connected with the county of Somerset*, 3 vols (1902)

Halket, S. and Laing, J. *A Dictionary of the Anonymous and Pseudonymous Literature of Great Britain*, 4 vols (1882–8)

Hewitt, R. G. *A Bibliography of Blackpool and the Fylde of Lancashire*, Library Association Fellowship thesis (1964)

Hodgson, H. W. *A Bibliography of the History and Topography of Cumberland and Westmorland* (1968)

Humphreys, A. L. *A Handbook to County Bibliography; being a bibliography of bibliographies relating to the counties and towns of Great Britain and Ireland* (1917)

Liverpool Corporation, Library Museum and Arts Committee. *Liverpool Prints and Documents Catalogue* (1908)

Matthews, E. R. N. *Bristol Bibliography: a catalogue of the books, pamphlets, collectanea in the Central Reference Library* (1916)

Mayo, C. H. *Bibliotheca Dorsetiensis: being a carefully compiled account of printed books and pamphlets relating to the history and topography of the county of Dorset* (1885)

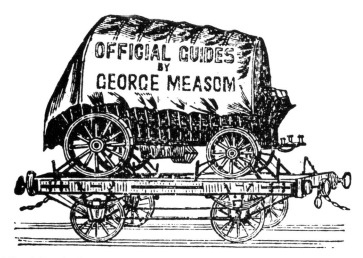

78. *The Official Illustrated Guide to the Great Western Railway:* device

Newcastle upon Tyne Public Libraries Committee. *Local Catalogue of Material Concerning Newcastle and Northumberland as Represented in the Central Public Library, Newcastle upon Tyne* (1932)

Norton, J. E. *Guide to the National and Provincial Directories of England and Wales, Excluding London, Published before 1856* (1950)

Ottley, G. *A Bibliography of British Railway History* (1965)

Reading Public Libraries. *Local Collection Catalogue of Books and Maps Relating to Berkshire* (1958), and *Supplement* (1967)

Smith, J. R. *Bibliotheca Cantiana: a bibliographical account of what has been published on the history, topography, antiquities, customs, and family genealogy, of the county of Kent* (1837)

Southport Public Libraries. *A Selection of General Works from the Local History Collection* (1967)

Walters, G. *The Tourist and Guide Book Literature of Wales 1770–1870*, University of Wales MSc thesis (1966)

79. *Black's Picturesque Guide to the English Lakes:* comparative views of lakes and comparative heights of mountains

COMPARATIVE VIEW OF LAKES

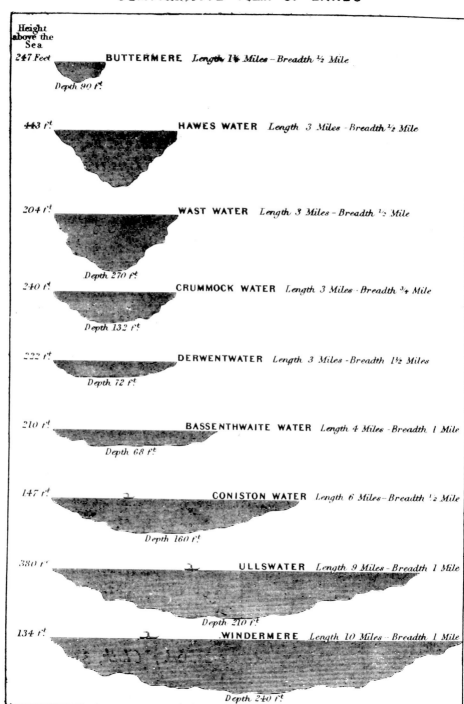

Height above the Sea

247 Feet   BUTTERMERE   *Length 1¼ Miles – Breadth ½ Mile*
Depth 90 f.ᵗ

443 f.ᵗ   HAWES WATER   *Length 3 Miles – Breadth ½ Mile*

204 f.ᵗ   WAST WATER   *Length 3 Miles – Breadth ½ Mile*
Depth 270 f.ᵗ

240 f.ᵗ   CRUMMOCK WATER   *Length 3 Miles – Breadth ¾ Mile*
Depth 132 f.ᵗ

322 f.ᵗ   DERWENTWATER   *Length 3 Miles – Breadth 1½ Miles*
Depth 72 f.ᵗ

210 f.ᵗ   BASSENTHWAITE WATER   *Length 4 Miles – Breadth 1 Mile*
Depth 68 f.ᵗ

147 f.ᵗ   CONISTON WATER   *Length 6 Miles – Breadth ½ Mile*
Depth 160 f.ᵗ

380 f.ᵗ   ULLSWATER   *Length 9 Miles – Breadth 1 Mile*
Depth 210 f.ᵗ

134 f.ᵗ   WINDERMERE   *Length 10 Miles – Breadth 1 Mile*
Depth 240 f.ᵗ

J. Bartholomew, Sc

COMPARATIVE HEIGHTS OF MOUNTAINS.

In this diagram it is not attempted to give the contour of the peaks but merely the relative heights

Scawfell Pike 3203

Scawfell 3162
Helvellyn 3118
Skiddaw 3058

Bowfell 2960 Great Gable 2949 Pillar 2927 Crossfell 2928

Fairfield 2862 Saddleback 2847
Grassmoor 2805

St Sunday Crag 2755
High Street 2718
Hart Crag 2697
Red Pike 2650
Coniston Old Man 2633 Grisedale Pike 2605
Glaramara 2560

Ill Bell 2476

Harrison Stickle 2401 ⎫
                      ⎬ Langdale Pikes
Pike o' Stickle 2323 ⎭

Carrock Fell 2173 High Pike 2165

Walna Scar 2035

Black Combe 1974

Mell Fell 1750

Honister Crag 1700

Wansfell 1581

Latrigg (Skiddaws Cub) 1203

Dent Hill 1130
Loughrigg Fell 1101

Penrith Beacon
937

Scilly Bank
530

WATERFALLS

Scale Force 156

Barrow Cascade 124

Lodore Cascade 100

Colwith Force 90

Airey Force 80
Dungeon Gill Force 80

Stock Gill Force 70

Birker Force 60
Stanley Gill Force 60
Sour Milk Force 60

Upper Fall Rydal 50

Skelwith Force 20

Index

N, B. *To find the Distance from any one Place to another, look along the Top*
last in Alphabetical Order look down the Side. Where the Lines meet, the L...
...le for...

												East Bourne	
												270	
												34	27
												328	7
												160	28
												97	25
												172	15
												80	28
												207	7
												76	28
												277	28
												107	21
												89	24
												247	24
												224	31
Tenby	244	80	142	235	266	130	313	185	126	336	287	26	
Tunbridge Wells	37	250	143	54	30	150	65	198	128	167	32	24	
Weymouth	128	187	67	95	122	65	205	230	110	258	149	27	
Worthing	59	180	112	15	11	130	107	220	138	193	40	27	
Yarmouth	125	288	234	184	183	225	198	210	201	38	184	24	